Sunset

Ideas for

STORAGE

BOOKSHELVES · CUPBOARDS · CABINETS

By the editorial staff of Sunset Books

LANE BOOKS · MENLO PARK, CALIFORNIA

PHOTOGRAPHER CREDITS

Aplin-Dudley Studios: 85 (lower left), 121 (lower right). William Aplin: 29 (upper right), 36 (lower left), 43 (left), 45 (upper right). Morley Baer: 10 (lower right), 67 (lower left, lower right). George Ballis: 27 (lower right). Nancy Bannick: 27 (lower center), 87 (lower left, lower right). Jerry Bragstad: 28 (upper left). Ernest Braun: 8 (upper right), 9 (bottom), 13 (upper right), 36 (lower center), 37 (upper left), 49 (lower right), 66 (lower left), 67 (upper, lower center), 95 (lower left, lower right), 103 (lower left, lower right), 114 (upper right). Building and Hardware News Photo: 75 (upper). Tom Burns, Jr.: 48 (lower left), 72 (lower right), 73. Carroll C. Calkins: 97. Camera Hawaii: 56 (lower left). Glenn M. Christiansen: 11 (lower right), 19 (lower right), 27 (lower left), 28 (upper right), 36 (lower right), 41 (lower center), 69 (lower right), 76 (upper), 81 (lower left), 86 (upper center, upper right), 88 (lower right), 101, 102 (upper left), 106 (lower left). Robert C. Cleveland: 48 (lower right). Robert Cox: 15 (upper left, upper right), 26 (lower left), 34 (lower left), 61 (lower right), 72 (upper), 80 (lower left), 112 (lower center, lower right). Dearborn-Massar: 34 (lower right), 35 (upper right), 40 (lower left, lower right), 52 (lower), 55 (upper right), 59, 72 (lower left), 85 (upper left, upper right), 99 (lower left, lower center, lower right), 107 (upper right), 115 (upper left). Alex de Paola: 107 (lower). Max Eckert: 61 (upper left), 78. Phil Fein & Associates: 68 (lower left). Richard Fish: 9 (upper left), 10 (upper), 17 (upper left), 18 (lower right), 24, 25 (upper left, upper right), 28 (lower right), 29 (upper left), 31 (upper left, lower right), 32 (upper left, upper right, lower left), 33 (lower left), 34 (lower center), 35 (upper left), 36 (upper left), 44 (lower left, lower right), 45 (lower left), 48 (upper left), 55 (lower right), 56 (lower right), 57 (upper right), 61 (lower left, lower center), 66 (lower right), 77 (lower right), 84, 86 (lower left, lower right), 87 (upper left, upper right), 88 (lower left), 92 (lower right), 93 (upper left), 99 (upper left, upper right), 103 (upper right), 112 (upper right), 117. Frank L. Gaynor: 47 (upper left), 89 (lower left), 92 (lower left). Elizabeth Green: 95 (upper right). Dean D. Hesketh Photography: 9 (lower right), 13 (lower left). D. U. Higgins: 114 (lower right). Art Hupy: 13 (lower right), 25 (lower right), 35 (lower right), 55 (lower left), 64, 94 (lower right), 113 (lower left). Roy Krell: 40 (upper left, upper right), 43 (right), 74 (upper left), 88 (upper right), 112 (lower left). Edmund Y. Lee: 27 (upper left, upper right), 57 (upper left), 61 (upper center), 79 (lower left, lower right), 111 (left). Martin Litton: 79 (upper left, upper right). Masonite Corporation: 25 (lower left). Michael McGinnis: 16 (upper right). Morris Studio: 81 (upper right). Nelson/Zellers Photo: 102 (lower left). Don Normark: 11 (upper right), 19 (lower left), 29 (upper right), 32 (lower right), 33 (upper), 35 (lower left), 36 (upper right), 41 (lower left), 49 (upper left, upper right), 61 (upper right), 66 (upper left), 69 (upper left, upper right), 75 (lower right), 77 (upper left), 89 (upper right), 92 (upper right), 94 (upper right), 98 (lower left, lower right), 103 (upper left), 106 (lower right). Kent Oppenheimer: 47 (lower right), 68 (upper left, upper right), 94 (upper left). Maynard L. Parker: 44 (upper right). Charles R. Pearson: 39, 41 (upper right), 45 (lower right), 57 (lower right), 98 (upper right). Photo-Craft Co.-Hawaii: 26 (upper left, upper right), 44 (upper left), 53 (upper), 54 (lower). George E. Peterson: 66 (upper right). Gerald Ratto: 10 (lower left). Tom Riley: 15 (lower left, lower center), 20 (upper right, lower right), 55 (upper left), 76 (lower left), 80 (lower right), 109, 111 (right), 113 (lower center), 118, 119, 120 (lower left, lower right). Joseph Risinger: 26 (lower center, lower right). John Robinson: 98 (upper left). Martha Rosman: 37 (lower left, lower right), 49 (lower left), 56 (upper left, upper right), 74 (upper right, lower), 89 (upper left, upper center, lower center, lower right), 102 (upper right), 112 (upper left), 115 (lower left, lower right). Julius Shulman: 12 (lower), 18 (lower left), 114 (upper left, lower left), 115 (upper right). Douglas M. Simmonds: 47 (lower right), 77 (upper right), 85 (lower right). Blair Stapp: 80 (upper left), 121 (lower left). Shan Stewart: 13 (upper left), 14 (upper right). Margaret Stovall: 18 (upper left, upper right). Hugh N. Stratford: 14 (lower right), 76 (lower right). Henry F. Unger: 108 (upper left, upper right). Darrow M. Watt: 16 (upper left, lower left, lower right), 17 (upper right), 19 (upper left), 28 (lower left), 29 (upper center, lower left), 30 (lower right), 31 (lower left), 52 (upper), 53 (lower), 54 (upper), 57 (lower left), 65 (upper left, upper right), 81 (upper right, lower right), 92 (upper left), 93 (lower left, lower right), 94 (lower left), 102 (lower right), 106 (upper), 108 (lower left, lower right), 113 (upper left, upper right), 121 (upper). Ray O. Welch: 75 (lower left). R. Wenkam: 8 (upper left), 9 (upper right, lower left), 11 (upper left, lower left), 17 (lower left, lower center), 21 (upper right), 29 (lower right), 30 (upper, lower left), 31 (upper right), 33 (lower right), 34 (upper left, upper right), 37 (upper right), 41 (upper left, lower right), 48 (upper right), 60, 65 (lower left, lower right), 95 (upper left), 107 (upper left).

Cover: Courtesy of Western Wood Products Association.

Edited by Sherry Gellner

Twelfth Printing July 1972

All rights reserved throughout the world. Second Edition. Copyright © 1966 by Lane Magazine & Book Company, Menlo Park, California. L. C. No. 66-24884. Title No. 638. Lithographed in U. S.

CONTENTS

INTRODUCTION: Planning Your Storage 4

IDEAS:

Books and Magazines 6
Kitchen Supplies 22
Glassware and Dinnerware 38
Linens 42
Bathroom Supplies 46
Laundry and Cleaning Supplies 50
Sewing Equipment 58
Clothing 62
Children's Clothing, Toys 70
Hi-fi, Records, Television 82
Household Office Supplies 90
Firewood 96
Bottled Wines 100
Home Workshops 104
Bulky Items 110
Garden Tools and Supplies 116

CONSTRUCTION HINTS:

Selecting and Installing Units 122
Counter Tops 123
Hinged Doors 124
Sliding Doors 124
Rolling Doors 124
Folding Doors 125
Cabinet Interiors 125
Building Between the Studs 128

PLANNING YOUR STORAGE

To those who have suffered from inadequate storage space in their homes for longer than they care to remember, the addition of as many new storage units as possible may seem the best solution. But unfortunately, this is not so simple. Lining every room in your house with cabinets and closets may give you plenty of space, but it subtracts from the living area and it still may not satisfy all your storage needs. Only with careful planning and arrangement will you reach a satisfactory situation in which you have enough storage space.

Storage, like the rest of your home, is personal—an expression of your talent and taste. The best storage is the arrangement that contributes the most to making your family's living habits as pleasant as possible. For this reason, don't approach the problems involved in terms of rigid imitation of what was done somewhere else. Instead, use your imagination and planning skill to work out a storage system that provides a practical solution to your particular needs.

You will find helpful ideas in this book. By adapting principles and ideas to your own particular needs, you can better judge the storage provisions in a new home, plan for more space in a remodel, or convert inadequate facilities to functional, organized units suited to your needs.

Finding storage space without extensive remodeling

The first step in planning storage is to decide just exactly what is needed—what items are to be stored, the amount of space necessary. There is no short-cut to determine this. You will have to sit down with pencil and paper and figure it out.

After you have outlined what new storage facilities are needed, you are faced with the problem of finding space in which to put them. The difficulties can be solved if your new home is still on the drawing board. If you are remodeling, the problem also is not too serious, since you can control the design of the remodeled area.

It is when new storage space must be added without benefit of remodeling that the space problem is critical. Here are some suggestions for approaching this situation:

Re-organize existing storage units. Re-organization of cabinet and closet interiors many times can open up space that is inadequately used. For example: the addition of adjustable shelves, or the conversion of shelving to trays or drawers may double the storage space within a unit.

You can also improve present facilities by using commercially manufactured accessories. The number and types of accessories and gadgets for storage units increases every day. There is a special hook, rack, stand, pull-out, rod, or hanger to accommodate almost every item that does not fit conveniently on a shelf or in a drawer. Fortunately, most accessories are available in a wide variety of sizes or are adjustable. Regardless of the depth of a closet or the width of a cabinet, you can usually find an accessory to fit.

Replace old cabinets. If the appearance or usefulness of old storage units is completely unsatisfactory, they can be replaced with new cabinets that will serve you better. This replacement of the old with the new, larger, more convenient storage cabinets may eliminate the need for additional storage units.

Add cabinets or closets in unused space. All areas out of traffic lanes and not being put to good use can be converted to some sort of storage; every open wall is a potential storage wall or foundation for shelves or cabinets. A door can be outlined by built-in bookcases. The wall space below a window can be converted to a low storage cabinet. An alcove or similar wall irregularity can be filled with a closet. A room can be divided into two rooms by the installation of a storage room divider.

Re-arrange furniture to open up wall space. The re-arrangement of furniture or removal of paintings or other decorations may open up wall space for the addition of new storage units.

You may also be able to use free-standing storage cases as pieces of furniture. If well constructed and finished properly, cabinets and storage chests can be arranged to match other furnishings. By attaching legs to a cabinet and using finished wood in construction, it can be used as an end table; by covering a low chest with a cushion and material, it can become a window seat; cabinets for hi-fidelity music equipment many times can be examples of fine craftsmanship.

All of these suggestions may not be applicable in your home, but the principles are. If you absolutely must have more storage space, cast a shewd eye about the house in search of areas that can be converted to storage. If you've been looking for an opportunity to rearrange a room without actually remodeling, this may be your chance. Your own ingenuity and adaptability of ideas is usually the determining factor in whether you find the storage space you need.

The use of combination units

Multi-purpose storage units that appear to be a single fixture but actually are a combination of many different ideas are rapidly becoming part of today's new homes. Examples of these units are: the music wall, which may house hi-fidelity equipment, the television set, record player, tape recorder, and record albums; the bedroom storage wall, including clothes rods, shoe racks, drawers, shelves, cabinets, and a vanity.

If you decide in favor of a combination unit, be sure to think of it as a collection of small, separate units under a single roof. Each individual cabinet or shelf should be specifically designed for a particular type of storage. A multi-purpose unit that is planned as only a catch-all usually winds up as an inefficiently used hodge-podge of odds and ends that does nothing to encourage neatness or efficient use of space.

The use of built-ins

This popular storage method obtains the maximum amount of storage space with a minimum sacrifice of living area. Built-ins are permanent elements of room design whether they hug the wall or are built-in as part of the house structure. Here are some advantages of using built-ins:

Units can be disguised or hidden. If the room calls for hidden storage units, built-ins can have doors that match solid walls, invisible hinges, and unobtrusive door handles or pulls. Even if the units are attached snugly to an existing structure and project into the room, they can be finished to blend with their surroundings.

Size and shape are variable. Built-in units can be designed to compensate for the deficiencies of any room. Blank wall space in some cases can be completely eliminated. This is especially true when room dividers are made up entirely of storage units.

Construction costs can be lowered. If only the front of a built-in unit is visible, this is the only place where finished materials are required. Also, since the attachment to walls or floor takes advantage of the room's basic structural strength, it may be possible to use a lighter grade of lumber and still have adequate support.

How to use this book

Perhaps the most important feature of functional storage is that the facilities are designed to meet specific needs. The following chapters discuss 16 different types of storage and what facilities are best to accommodate them. When planning storage units for your home, study the ideas and principles that have worked for others. Similar designs could very well help you solve your storage problems.

The final section of the book provides construction pointers for the handyman who would like to build any of the various types of facilities presented. By combining these helpful hints with the ideas presented, you can best determine the most practical and workable solution for eliminating any storage dilemmas in your home.

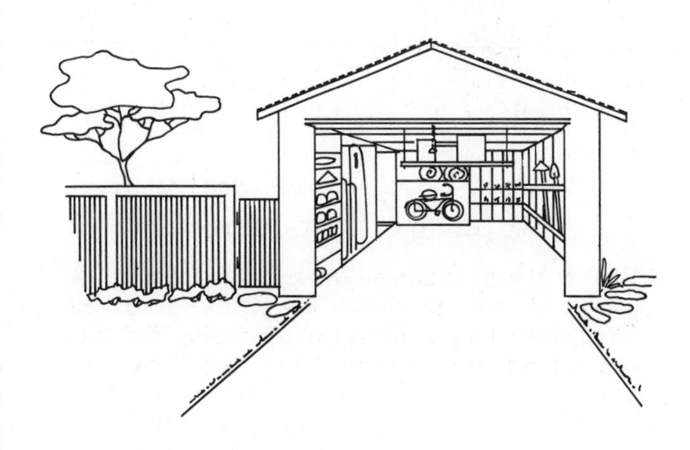

Storage for

BOOKS AND MAGAZINES

Location for bookshelves • Shelf sizes • Vertical and horizontal shelves

Ceiling- or wall-attached shelves • Concealed or open shelf supports

Portable bookcases • Displaying and storing magazines

Almost every household has a collection—large or small—of books and magazines. This collection may be large enough to fill an entire wall of book shelving, or it may consist of just a few carefully selected favorites. Whatever the case may be, providing for book and magazine storage can add to the design, comfort, and atmosphere of any room.

If you have bookcases just sufficient for your present collection, where do you put new acquisitions? How should you plan for size and depth of shelves? How can you use the decorative quality of books and magazines to best advantage? What if you've recently moved into a house and are planning book storage from scratch? Here are some suggestions for making books and magazines readily available:

Bookshelves can go anywhere

There is no standard location for bookshelves, just as there is no standard design. They may be free-standing, built-in to fill an open corner or unused section of wall, used as a floor-to-ceiling room divider, or combined with music equipment.

The living room or den may provide the most free wall space of any room in the house. Comfortable chairs or sofa may be the enticing factor here. Of course, noise from family activities may be a distracting feature, but being within earshot can be important to families with small children. Bookcases hung high on a wall avoid complications of furniture arrangement. They also bring color and pattern to eye level. Bookcases placed low on a wall leave space for wall hangings or paintings. If you concentrate your books on one wall of the living room, you can gain a strong decorative element and make your room warm and inviting.

The bedroom may be a more practical location for bookshelves. If your pleasure reading is done in the hours before retiring, this location is ideal for being away from children and the television set. Perhaps the bookcase can frame a window, be built into the wall above a desk, or be conveniently placed within arm's reach of a comfortable chair. Commercially-made headboards can be obtained with sufficient shelving to accommodate several books. For those who like to read in bed, this arrangement provides handy storage.

In children's rooms, bookcases may be combined effectively with general storage units. Shelves can be built above the study area or as part of the wardrobe closet. When planning book storage for children, keep in mind that their books often differ in size from adult books. Adjustable shelving may be the answer for adapting the bookcases to fit a wide range of book sizes.

Most books fit two shelf sizes

Most volumes measure 8 to 10½ inches in height and about 5½ to 8½ inches in width. Therefore, bookshelf space should be a minimum of 9 inches high and 8 inches deep for books of average size. For larger volumes, a shelf 12 inches deep and 12 inches high will be adequate. Width of the shelving depends on the amount of wall space you have available and the number of volumes to be stored. Estimate 8 to 10 average-sized books to each running foot of shelf.

Plan for easy reaching when adding bookshelves. The shelf 72 to 76 inches off the floor will probably be the highest the woman of the house can reach without standing on a chair. However, if you are planning for a storage wall that will reach the ceiling, the top shelves can be fitted with doors for bulk storage cabinets, or used as niches to display pieces of sculpture.

The three or four lowest shelves also may be inconvenient for you. General storage cabinets built in the lower 30 inches of the bookcase may be very practical. Or you may want to convert this

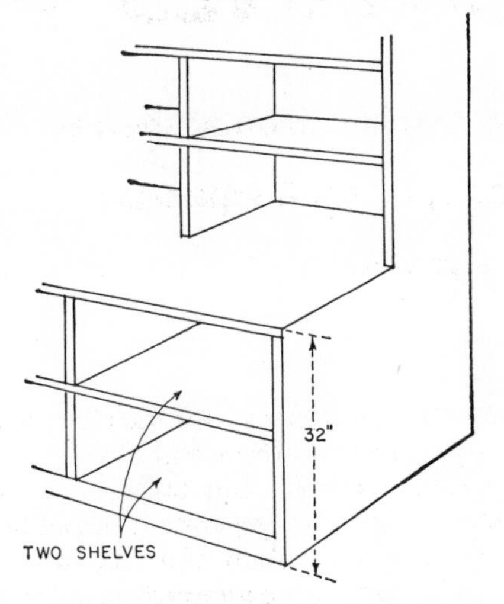

Lower shelves can form counter top

space to deep shelving for atlases, photo albums, and other large volumes. This arrangement also forms a counter top for work or browsing (see drawing above).

How to keep magazines tidy

Magazines seldom are read in one sitting. They tend to fall where they're used—on tables, desks, chairs, counters—so they'll be handy to pick up again later on. Unfortunately, this temporary convenience often results in a long-term inconvenience as more magazines and other items are piled one on another. Prompt action is the key to keeping the magazine storage problem in hand. As new issues come into the house, get rid of the ones you are through with as soon as possible.

Flat storage of magazines usually presents no problems. The main point is to keep the shelves wide and deep enough to handle the largest magazines to be stored. Just measure the issues that come into your home every week or month and design your storage units to fit these issues.

Tilted shelves that expose titles offer another popular and easy solution to storing magazines. The shelves can be used for either magazines or paperbound books. The supports (not shown in the drawing) are wooden triangles.

This type of shelving can be placed in regular bookcases or you can convert an entire section of wall to magazine storage. Not only will this keep

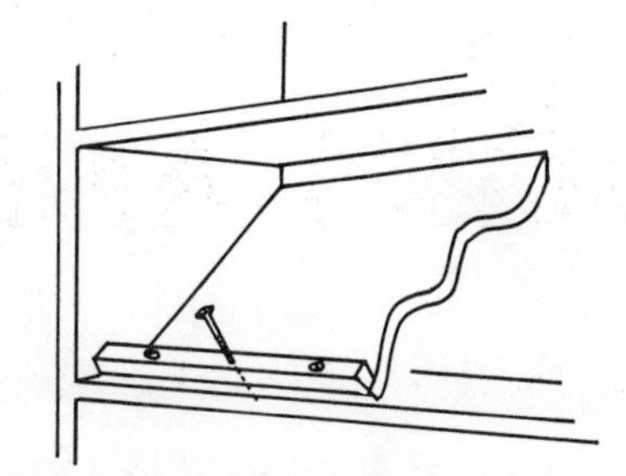
Tilted shelves for displaying magazines

order, but the changing covers give you a bright addition of color to the room.

Vertical racks can store a surprisingly large number of magazines while taking up a minimum of space. A rack can be made to fit into even the narrowest

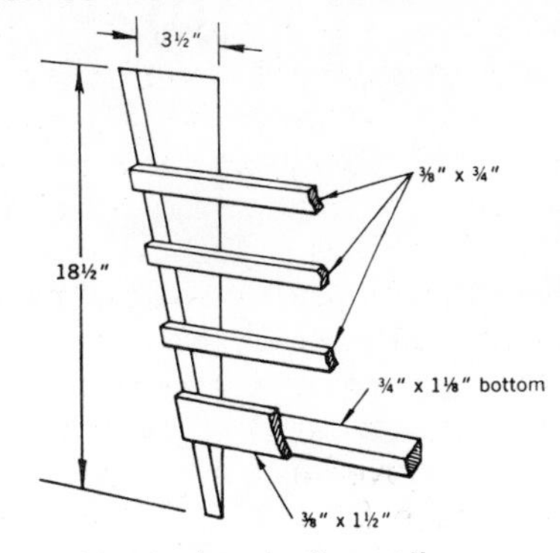

Vertical racks fit small areas

unused wall section. Sections of the rack are stacked (and nailed) one over another. The bottom piece has one edge cut on a slant to match the angle of the slanting side pieces.

Magazine binders—available through many publishing companies—will hold either 6 or 12 issues.

The specifications for this binder are for 12 issues of *Sunset* magazine. For other sizes, alter the dimensions and spacing of wires. Although plywood covers will keep magazines neat and will stand up through long use, you may find that laminated plastic will be adequate for your needs.

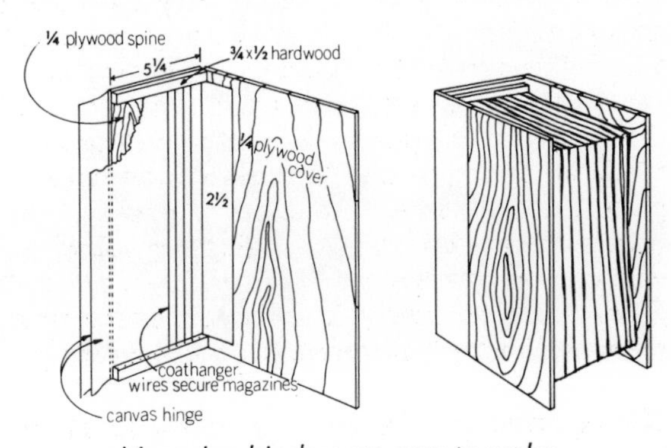

Magazine binders are easy to make

Books can go anywhere

IN FREE-STANDING SHELVES

These free-standing shelves screen the living room from deck. Low ledge serves as seat. Arch.: Vladimir Ossipoff.

IN TWO-STORY STAIRWELL

Bookshelf walls soaring upward in a two-story stairwell provide a striking background. Design: John I. Matthias.

AROUND LIVING ROOM HEARTH

The depth of a raised brick hearth is utilized for bookshelves in this light and airy living room. Lower shelves are used for displaying and storing magazines. Note the music speaker on upper shelf. Arch.: Henrik Bull.

IN STUDY OR GUEST ROOM

A wide variety of books is placed above this spare sofa bed with slanting headboard. Design: Harold Sylvester.

ABOVE BEDROOM HALL CABINETS

Shelves added above bedroom hall cabinets hold new acquisitions to this library. Arch.: Vladimir Ossipoff.

IN BEDROOM HALLWAY

Decorated with bookshelves and comfortable chair, large hallway serves as small study. Arch.: Vladimir Ossipoff.

IN CORNER OF FAMILY ROOM

Comfortable chairs, and books on open shelves in quiet corner invite leisurely reading. Archs.: Bissell & Duquette.

You can use available space or remodel

BOOKSHELVES EMPHASIZE HOUSE DESIGN

Hundreds of books line this living room wall with section posts helping to emphasize 8-foot module of house design. Light, comfortable chairs and fireplace make pleasant place for reading. Archs.: Holmes & Sellery.

UNUSED FIREPLACE REMOVED FOR BOOKSHELVES

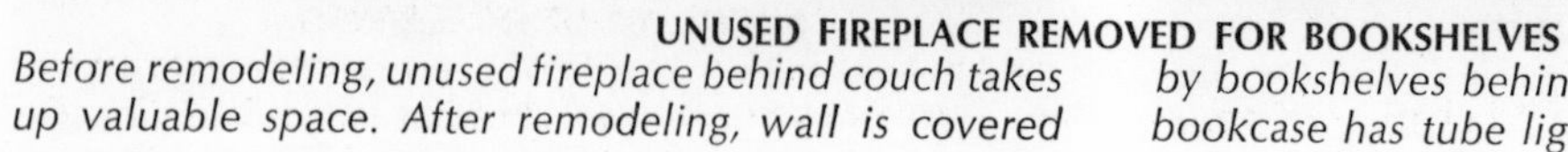

Before remodeling, unused fireplace behind couch takes up valuable space. After remodeling, wall is covered by bookshelves behind 12-foot-long sofa. Cove above bookcase has tube lighting. Archs.: Marquis and Stoller.

STORAGE ALONG A WINDOW WALL
Books line top of storage cabinets in small living room; screened vents provide fresh air. Arch.: Harry W. Seckel.

IT'S NO LONGER DEAD SPACE
Dead space under stairs serves well for adjustable book shelves. Longest shelf is 7 feet. Design: Jack McLin.

Good lighting and comfortable chairs are essential

A GOOD READING LIGHT
Free-standing unit combines seating, desk, catalog file drawer, large reading lamp. Arch.: Vladimir Ossipoff.

BOOKS WITHIN EASY REACH
Low shelves, within easy reach of comfortable chair, leave wall free for paintings. Archs.: Walker & McGough.

For versatile book storage

THEY ARE VERTICAL AND VARIABLE

Varying sizes of openings in vertical bookshelves accommodate many book sizes; arranging books is made easier. Unused portions hold tall decorative objects. There is enough room between units for cleaning and painting.

BOOKCASES ARE COMBINED WITH BUILT-IN CABINETS

Design of bookcases gives a strong horizontal line to the wall of this living room. Combined with built-in cabinets and desk, the bookshelves also become an important decorative element in room. Arch.: Gregory Ain.

Attached to ceiling or wall

HUNG FROM CEILING
Shelves of 1 by 1-inch surfaced redwood are supported by 1 by 1's on side of ceiling beams. Arch.: Bryce I. Cann.

SHELVES ON THREADED RODS
Supported by 5/8-inch threaded rods, each shelf rests on nut, washer; rods hang on hooks. Design: David Tucker.

SHELF STRIPS ATTACHED TO WALL
Upper part of wall in study is equipped with shelf strips, brackets to hold books. Archs.: Bissell & Duquette.

ADJUSTABLE SHELVES ON BRACKETS
A library wall is created with shelves in varying lengths hung on brackets; additional shelves can be added.

Shelf supports can be concealed or in the open

CONCEALED TRACKS SUPPORT BRACKETS
Concealed tracks support adjustable brackets for 10-foot-long, shelves. Arch.: Alexander C. Prentice.

NAILS CONCEALED IN WALL
Carefully placed so as to appear virtually concealed, simple nails hold shelves to wall. Archs.: Jones & Emmons.

IRON RODS ARE PART OF DECOR
Wrought iron rods (outer end is flattened, other end grouted in hole) hold shelves. Arch.: Alfred Johnson.

ALUMINUM BRACKETS FIT OVER PARTITION
Aluminum brackets fit over partition, support shelves without piercing wall. Arch.: Lawrence G. Waldron.

Portable bookcases—easy to install—easy to move

A PORTABLE BOOKCASE FOR A PORTABLE LIBRARY

Light enough to screw onto a wall, this portable bookcase holds compact paperback books. Top and bottom boxes are attached to wall; center one is removable. Mount with space between for extra shelves.

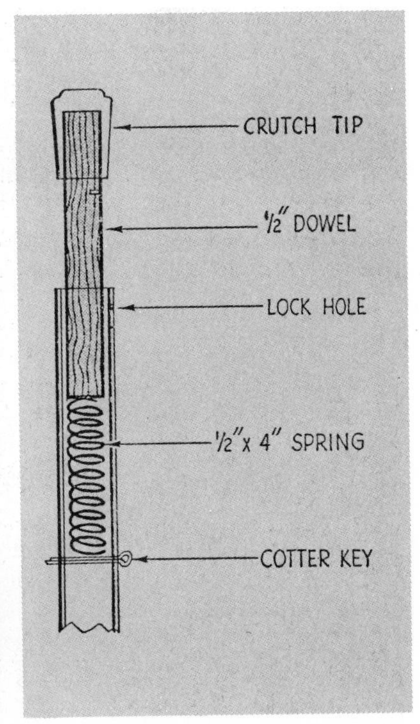

SPRING-LOADED ENDS HOLD BOOKSHELF IN PLACE

This bookshelf rests snugly against a wall without any fastenings. Four long tubes, spring loaded at top, push against ceiling. Shelves rest on 1-inch cotterpins. Dowels are cut to clear ceiling with springs ends compressed.

This bookcase comes apart for moving or storing

EASY TO MOVE ABOUT OR STORE

Lightweight but strong, bookcase is held together with dowels. Filled with books, it's very sturdy, but can be anchored to wall for additional support. Disassembled, it is easy to move; takes up very little space when stored.

These bookcases open for additional storage

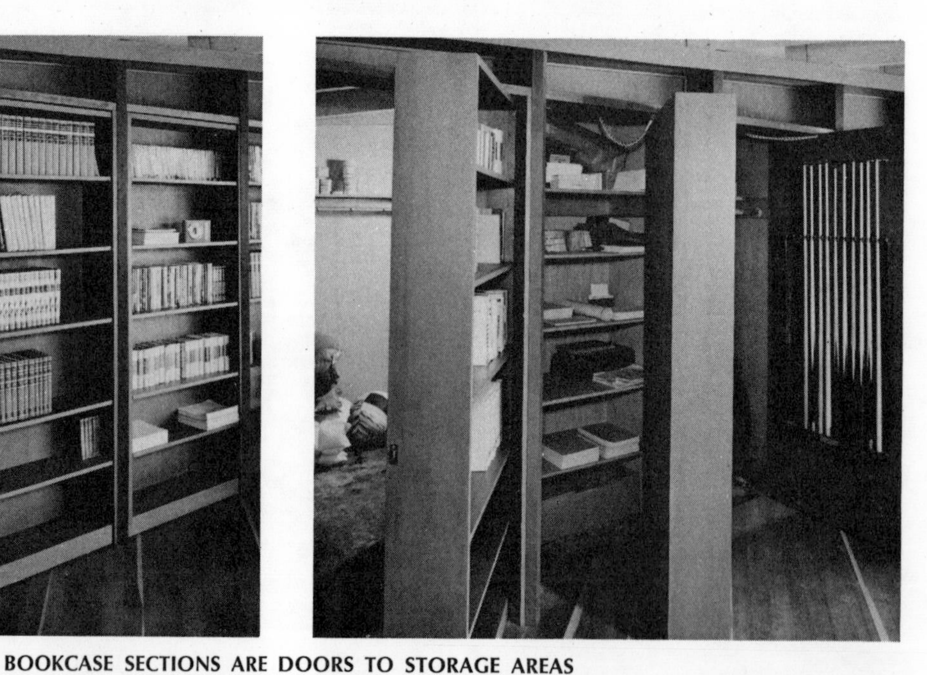

BOOKCASE SECTIONS ARE DOORS TO STORAGE AREAS

Bookcase wall in pool-side cabana offers shelf space for expanding book collection. Sections open to additional storage. Left to right: Access to pool equipment; deep shelf storage; large guest closet. Arch.: J. Martin Rosse.

Ideas for people who like to read in bed

SLANTED HEADBOARD FOR READING
Slanting headboard opens for blanket, pillow storage; books within easy reach. Design: Harold Sylvester.

PULL-OUT BOARDS BESIDE EACH BED
Pull-out boards, indirect lighting, and custom-built back rests for bed reading. Arch.: Morgan Stedman.

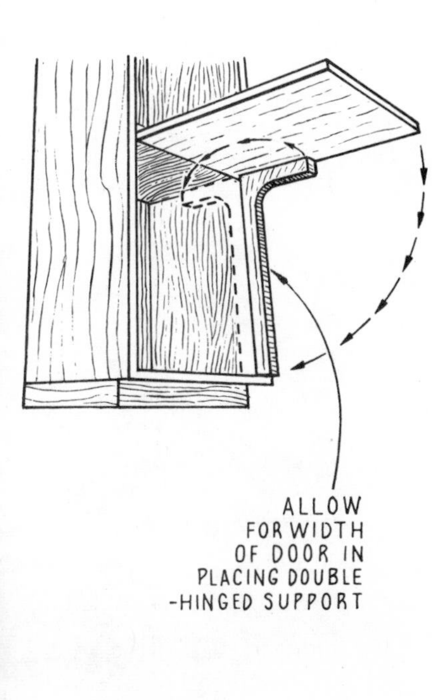

HEADBOARD IS COMPACT NIGHT-READING UNIT
Two panels swing out to form back rest and table; books and light are easy to reach. Closed, panels conceal storage space for bedside phone, blankets, pillow. Sketch shows how gate leg brace supports panel. Design: Paul D. Jones.

Ideas for displaying and storing magazines

DISPLAY SHELVES OPEN TO STORAGE SHELVES

Display shelves built in two piano-hinged cabinets, their ends angled where they meet so they will open without colliding. Cabinets open to reveal shelves. Perforated hardboard allows air circulation. Arch.: Jean Driskel.

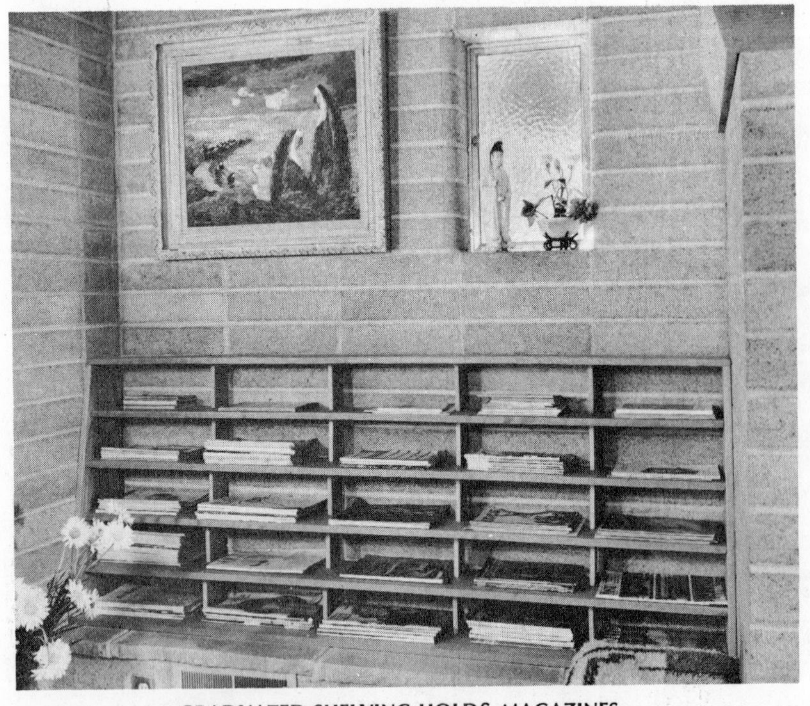

GRADUATED SHELVING HOLDS MAGAZINES

Ranging from 6-inch width at top to 12-inch at bottom, shelving holds large number of magazines; repeats block pattern. Design: William Alexander.

ROOM-DIVIDER CABINETS

Magazine cabinet serves as room divider. Arch.: Paul Sterling Hoag.

Racks can be simple and easy to build

MAGAZINE RACK CAN BE EXPANDED
Simple magazine rack, 5 feet long, 2 feet high, can be expanded in 2½-foot modules. Design: C. A. Powell, Jr.

FOR DISPLAY AND STORAGE
Simple, sturdy magazine case permits colorful display of current issues and ample storage of back numbers.

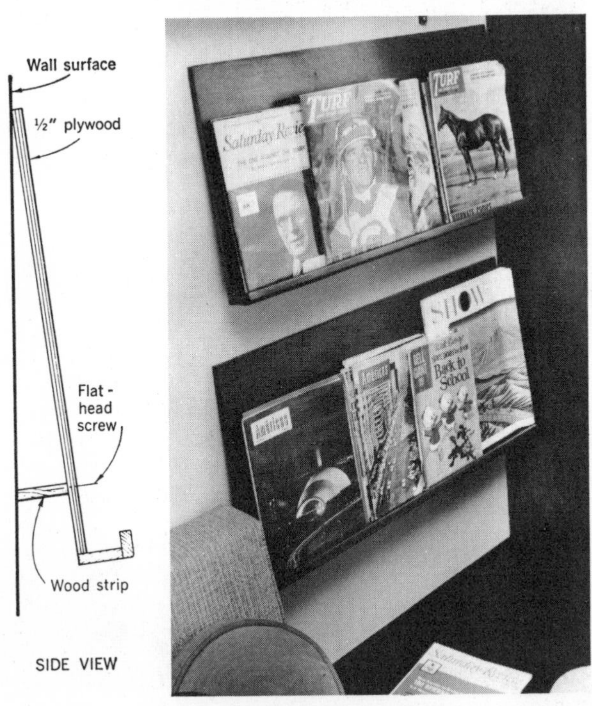

NAILED OR SCREWED TO WALL
Slanted plywood racks for the display of periodicals can be nailed or screwed to the wall. Arch.: Edward J. Baar.

RACK FITS INTO SMALL WALL SECTION
Made of Philippine mahogany, rack is glued and nailed together, nailed to trim. Design: Dr. Russell V. Lee.

Nailed to the wall...

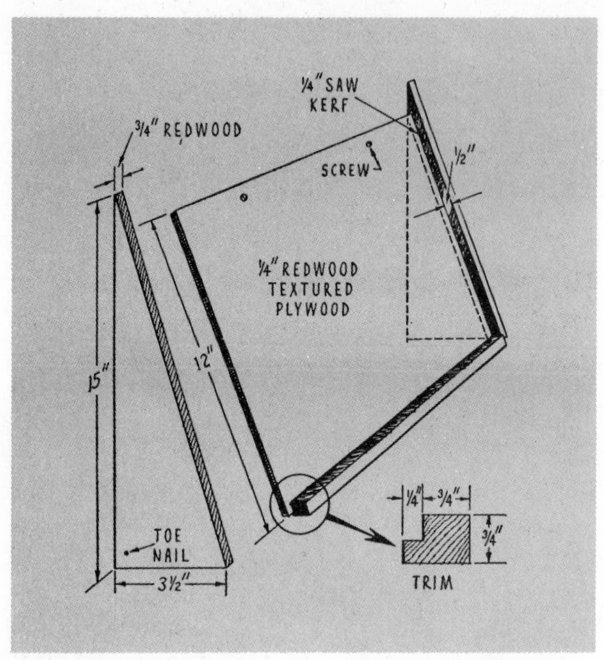

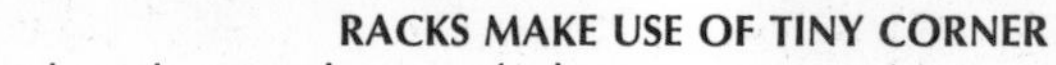

RACKS MAKE USE OF TINY CORNER

These racks decorate and make good use of door-cramped corner, with two display racks for current magazines and a bin-type rack for storage. Plan shows upper racks; lower bin juts out 1 1/2 inches farther.

Supported by brackets...

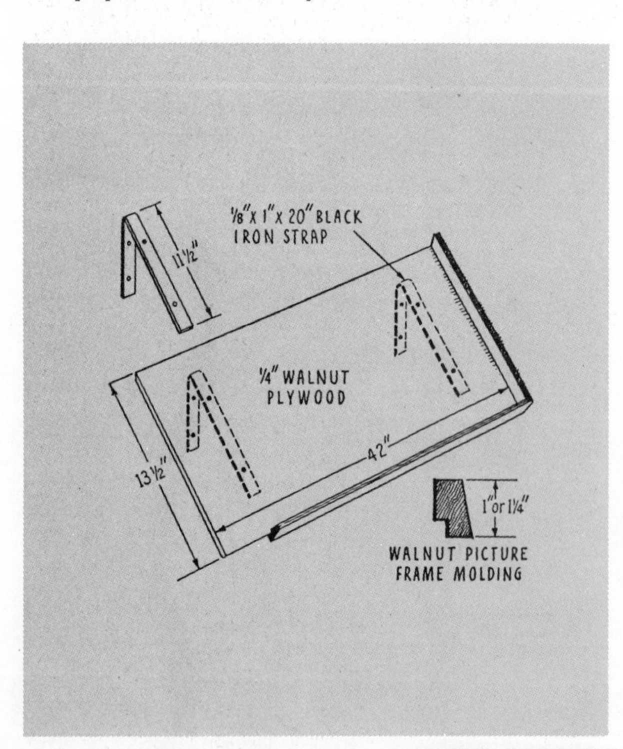

WELL-SUPPORTED BY METAL BRACKETS

Racks, trimmed with picture frame molding, are hung on wall by metal brackets. Walnut plywood and molding are glued together and nailed only on underside. Molding is mitered at two corners, brackets bent to 40° angle.

This rack fits against the end of a couch

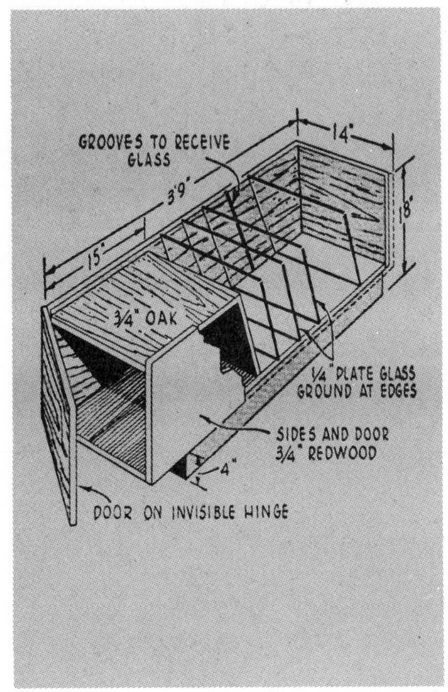

FRONT SECTION ENCLOSED FOR MISCELLANEOUS STORAGE

Magazines slide in between glass partitions in magazine rack snugly fitted at end of couch. Front is enclosed for miscellaneous storage. With door on invisible hinge, appearance of case is not marred. Arch.: Alfred Preis.

This portable magazine holder is easy to build

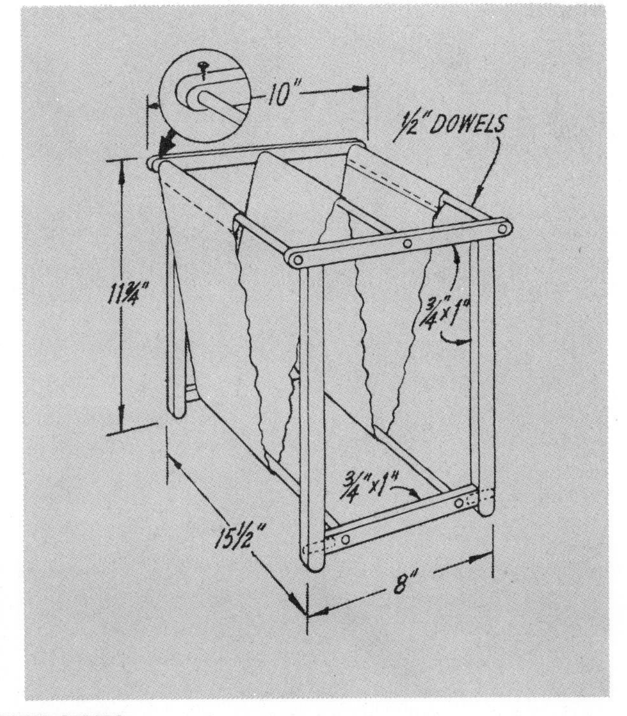

MADE OF BIRCH STRIPS

This portable magazine holder is made of birch strips, 1/2-inch dowels, and a 4-foot remnant of cloth. Cradle (note sketch) can be removed for laundering. For gayer effect, use colored material. Design: Robert Tanner.

Storage for

KITCHEN SUPPLIES

Convenience of pantries • Size of pantry units • Convenient silver storage

Appliance storage centers • Storage for breakfast appliances • Pots and pans

Hide-a-ways for bulky appliances • Handy storage for herbs and spices

The greatest of faults in home planning, according to builders, is the tendency to overcrowd the kitchen. When you consider that the kitchen is usually a rather small room to start with, and that appliances and accessories swallow a large portion of what space there is, it is obvious that kitchen storage calls for good planning—and ingenuity.

As with any room, appearance is certainly an important factor in kitchen planning. But—perhaps more than any room in the house—the problem of "what goes where" for handiness and working ease is extremely important.

Shopping schedule determines storage need

There is no sure-fire way of determining how much food storage is needed in a home. Actually, your shopping schedule is more important than the size of your family when it comes to determining food storage needs. For those who shop two or three times a week, a minimum amount of space may be adequate. On the other hand, for those who shop only on payday and bring home a carload of groceries to last a week or two, considerable shelf space may be needed.

Storage for the convenience of the cook is often the best arrangement, but not always. Certain foods keep better when stored at a distance from heat and moisture. Here are some suggestions for storing foods that need not be refrigerated.

A pantry for quantity storage can be an ideal arrangement if you live a good distance from the grocery store. Most cabinet shelves around the work centers fill up rapidly with food used every day; therefore, it is wise to make special provisions for the extra canned or dry goods that have been picked up on sale or purchased in case lots.

Shelving should be shallow. Although standard kitchen cabinets have shelves 12 inches deep, a good depth for shelving in pantry units is about 8 inches. This depth allows for one or two-deep storage of cans and dry goods and eliminates removing several items to get to the one in the back. The shelves should be firmly supported on cleats or brackets. Width and height of the shelf openings depend on the size of the items to be stored. Depending on the type of buying done at different times of the year, the shelves can be moved to accommodate smaller or larger items.

The one exception to the rule of shallow storage in pantry units is if the pantry is limited to canned goods. Here, slightly sloping shelves can feed the cans one at a time to the front of the shelf. (A small piece of molding on the front of the shelf will keep cans from falling off.)

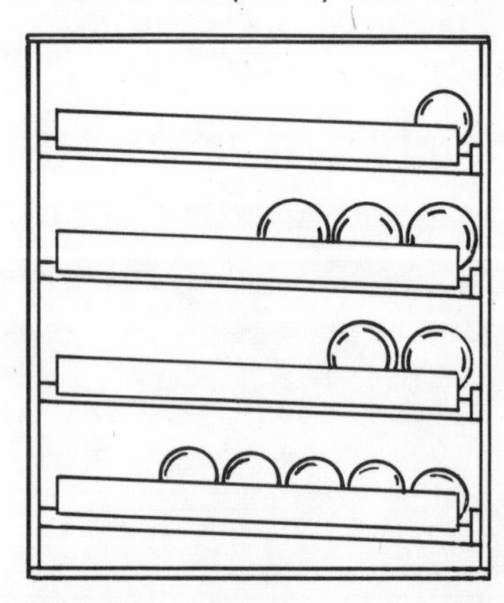

Cans roll to the front one by one

Keep herbs and spices air-tight. Every good cook has favorite spices that she likes to keep handy, usually close to the food preparation center and on open shelves where it's easy to read the labels. Ideally, spices should be stored away from heat, moisture, and light. Jar lids and can tops should be kept tightly closed to prevent the volatilization of the aromatic substances. If tightly covered, herbs will keep for about a year and a half, and ground spices for almost two years.

An auxiliary shelf between the regular cabinet shelves, or a spice cabinet set on the wall or on the counter beneath wall cabinets will be adequate storage room for most spices. Commercially-made units of this type are common, or you can easily build one to suit your needs.

Revolving spice racks are another popular way to store herbs and spices. These commercial devices are equipped with 2 or 3 tiers. The revolving shelves can make dead space in corner cabinets or other inaccessible spots usable.

Planning utensil storage

Storing kitchen utensils involves the same principles that are used with food. But with utensils, there are some complicating factors. Pots and pans are bulky, have handles that defy tidy storage, and have varying sized lids. Trays, cookie tins, and muffin tins, because of their peculiar shape, use up valuable shelf space if stored flat. Cutting tools must be protected to preserve their sharp edges and to eliminate the possibility of slicing your fingers. Portable appliances such as mixers and blenders become inconveniences if you have to move them from point of storage to point of use.

Whenever possible, make the storage unit fit the item to be stored. Above all, don't resort to stacking.

Store portable appliances adjacent to the work area and on the same level whenever possible. These valuable time and work savers *do* take up counter space but since most work done on a 24-inch-deep counter is toward the front, the rear portion can often be used for storage. Placed near an electrical outlet, you can then use flexible, roll-back doors or sliding doors to cover the appliance when not in use.

Pull-out, swing-out, or pop-up shelves can become an alternative solution to storing appliances on the work level. A base cabinet can store the appliance until it is needed. The shelf on which it is sitting is then raised, swung out, or lifted out and the appliance may be used at counter level. Hardware for this type of unit is available for installation.

Hang pots and pans—especially those used every day—to obtain the best functional storage. Storage should be close to the range in a space designed so that pots and pans can be hung on separate hooks.

Perforated hardboard attached to the wall above the range, or used to line a closet nearby, will keep these utensils readily accessible. Or, if you prefer, hooks installed on a wall or wood nailing strip can

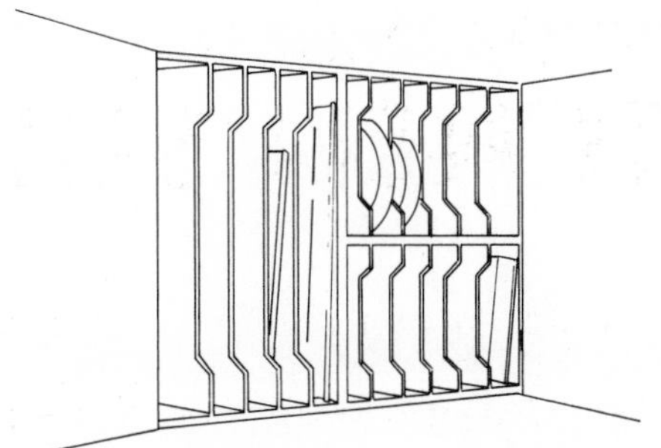

Vertical dividers permit easy removal

give you visible storage near the range or sink. Another solution is to attach the hooks on the bottom of an adjustable shelf.

Sliding brackets for pots and pans are commercially available. You can often place these brackets below counter-top ranges making these items easily accessible where they are most used.

Hooks or shallow racks are the best storage units for pot lids. You can purchase stock lid holders in varying sizes. However, you may prefer to use vertical dividers in a deep drawer.

Use vertical dividers for storing trays, cookie tins, and other flat pieces. Never stack these items. Vertical dividers in a cabinet or drawer, either set in grooves or held by cleats, will store a large

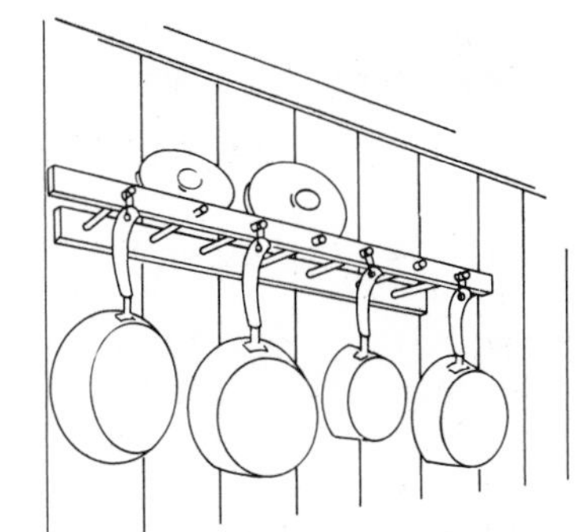

Pans hang on end of dowels

number of flat pieces. Be sure that the cabinet or drawer is deep enough to handle your largest trays. Also make sure that the storage unit will open far enough to permit easy removal of these utensils.

Store knives separately to protect the blades. Tossing your good knives into a drawer with other utensils is likely to nick and dull cutting edges. If you are remodeling or planning a new kitchen, you may want to consider the chopping block with slots conveniently placed for holding your knives vertically. An easier solution is to attach a slotted strip of wood to the bottom of a cabinet shelf. Another solution is to install a slotted strip of wood in a shallow drawer. The knives can be placed on edge in the slots in alternating positions.

For quantity storage—a pantry is very convenient

1 Close to point where supplies are unloaded, canned food rack is in hall just a step inside house.

2 Stock can easily be checked from delivery side; door is concealed panel in service hall.

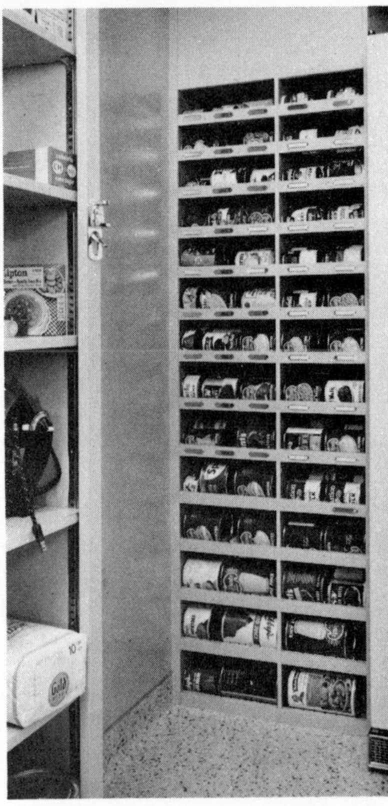

3 Pantry side is open, cans are easy to reach. Higher ones are identified by labels.

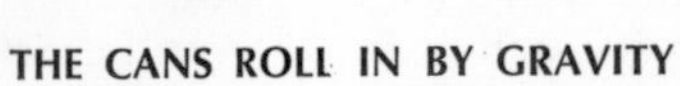

THE CANS ROLL IN BY GRAVITY

Canned goods are loaded from hallway onto gently inclined shelves, received inside pantry. Four-foot-long unit can accommodate case lots. Units can be made to fit available length. Design: Carl W. Johnson.

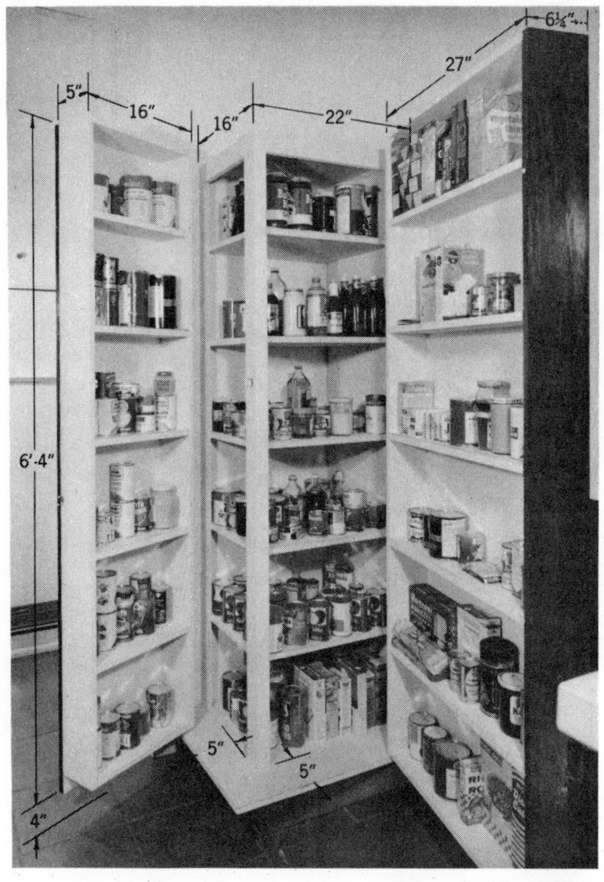

HALF THE STORAGE SPACE IS IN THE DOORS

Approximately half the storage space in this built-in pantry is on inside of the doors, making it easy to see and reach things. It's made of ¾-inch plywood, with 6-foot-4-inch doors on piano hinges. Archs.: Hyun and Whitney.

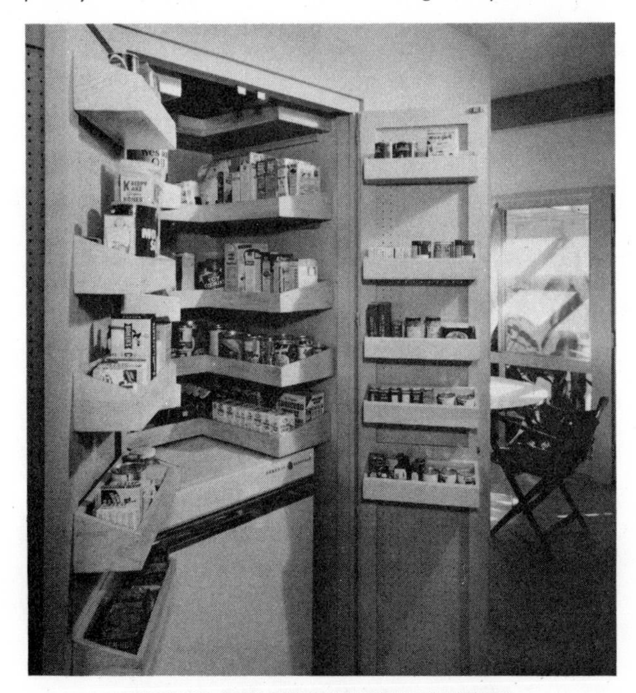

PANTRY AND FREEZER COMBINATION

Shelves hang on hooks in this pantry and freezer combination; can be adjusted to height of contents.

DIVIDED DOOR ON PANTRY-COOLER

Pantry and cooler sections of cupboard open separately; wire shelves are easy to clean. Arch.: William J. Bain, Jr.

Pantry units can be generous or pint-sized

THE ULTIMATE IN NARROW-SHELF STORAGE

Double outer doors have 6-inch shelves. Hinged inner storage cabinets with 4-inch shelves on each side open to reveal 8-inch fixed shelves. Pantry is 28 inches by 4 feet. Lip holds objects in place. Archs.: Morse and Tatom.

ONE-DEEP STORAGE

Storage cabinet acts as room divider. Archs.: Stedman & Williams.

FILL IN A CORNER . . . GAIN A PANTRY

This compact pantry fills in dining area corner. Shutter doors open at the front and side. Side opening is handy for canisters and other baking supplies.

SWING-OUT SHELVES REVEAL ADDITIONAL STORAGE

Space 4 feet wide and 2½ feet deep contains efficient food storage. Swing-out shelves allows for reaching staples that would be buried in back of single, wide shelf. Arch.: Groom, Blanchard, Lamen & MacCollin.

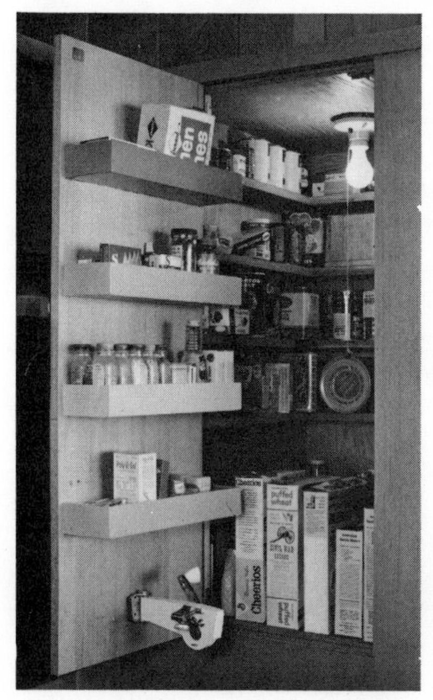

STORAGE ON FOUR WALLS

Shelves inside of door for storing small items. Design: David Tucker.

THERE'S NO ROOM FOR DOORS

Plastic roll-away cover closes pint-size pantry. Arch.: Alfred Preis.

A MINIATURE PANTRY

Small, open cupboard provides handy shelf space. Design: Earl D. Lyon.

How to keep your favorite spices handy

STORING SPICES IN A BLOCK OF WOOD
Spice rack is 2 by 3¾ by 47-inch piece of redwood, with 2-inch holes drilled in it on 2½-inch centers. Design: James P. Livingston.

BOARDS AND DOWELS
Redwood 1 by 3's are held together by ⅝-inch dowels; secured to wall by screws.

SHELF IS THREE INCHES WIDE
Metal jar tops are attached to underneath side with two screws (so lids won't turn). Jars spaced one inch apart.

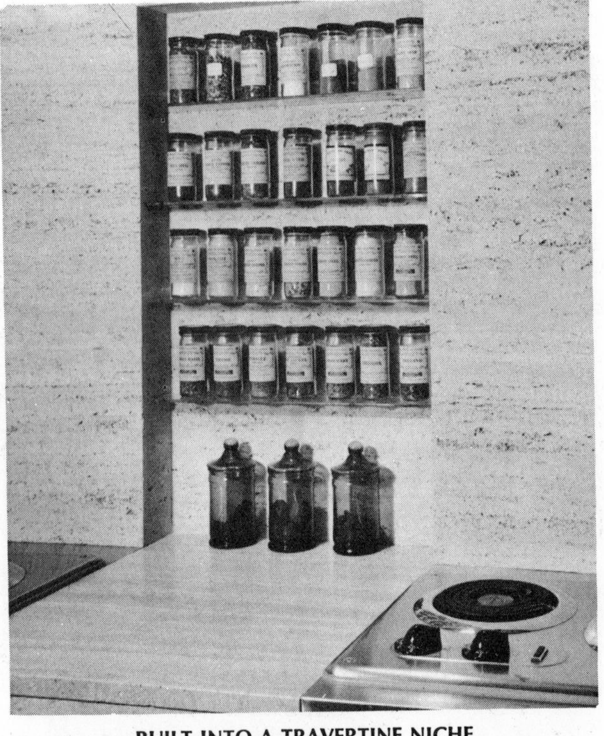

BUILT INTO A TRAVERTINE NICHE
Glass shelves fit into slots in niche above counter between table-top cooking units. Design: Fred Blair Green.

VERTICAL STORAGE
Spices are placed in narrow sections above range. Arch.: Russell Forester.

GLASS JARS STORE SPICES
Wide-mouthed glass jars with cork tops make colorful spice containers.

SPICES AT EYE LEVEL
Spices are above Meissen. Archs.: Edmundson, Kochendoerfer, Kennedy.

SHELVES OF 1 BY 1-INCH REDWOOD
Rack is suspended by screws from the cabinet above into the middle top horizontal member, and steadied with nails into studs behind.

PULL-OUT SHELVES
Narrow shelves pull out of cabinet, store spices, small items. Arch.: Edward Sullam.

Appliances can be stored in one center or separately

LIFT-UP PANEL COVERS APPLIANCE CENTER

Lift-up panel conceals this appliance center. Appliances are plugged in, pulled forward on counter for use. Even with panel closed, a single unit can be used by pulling cord through the cut-out in the bottom of panel.

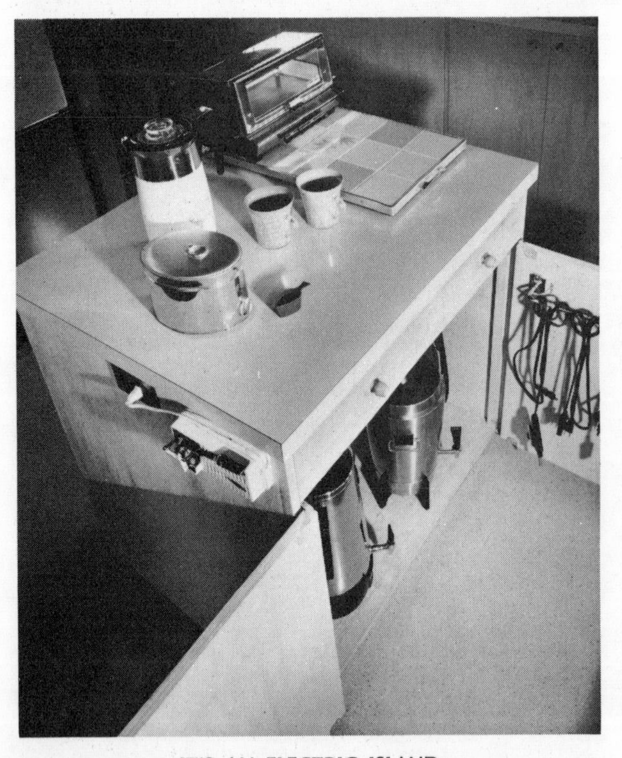

IT'S AN ELECTRIC ISLAND

Island is 3′ wide, 2′4″ deep, and makes a complete appliance center. Archs.: Lemmon, Freeth, Haines & Jones.

STORED IN CORNER OF COUNTER

Appliances are stored in corner generally inconvenient for working. Outlets in cabinet. Design: Janean.

AT END OF KITCHEN TABLE
Storage area for appliances at end of kitchen table is covered with bi-folding doors. Design: D. R. Robertson.

SMALL BUFFET NEAR KITCHEN TABLE
Cupboard space for appliances open toward table; clock-timer panel has outlets. Arch.: Vladimir Ossipoff.

SINGLE UNIT FOR BLENDER, MIXER
Power unit for blender and mixer is built into drawer; pull-out shelf stores accessories.

BLENDER AND MIXER BUILT INTO DRAWER
All accessories are stored alongside power unit built into drawer; outlet at back. Surface beneath unit is washable laminated plastic.

Handy storage for appliances used at breakfast

TOASTER CHAMBER
Piano-hinged top and end provide access to toaster, controls. Archs.: Hyun and Whitney.

TOAST AND COFFEE ON PULL-OUT SHELF
Pull-out shelf utilizes space in corner of kitchen; puts toaster and coffee pot conveniently near table. Design: Fred Blair Green.

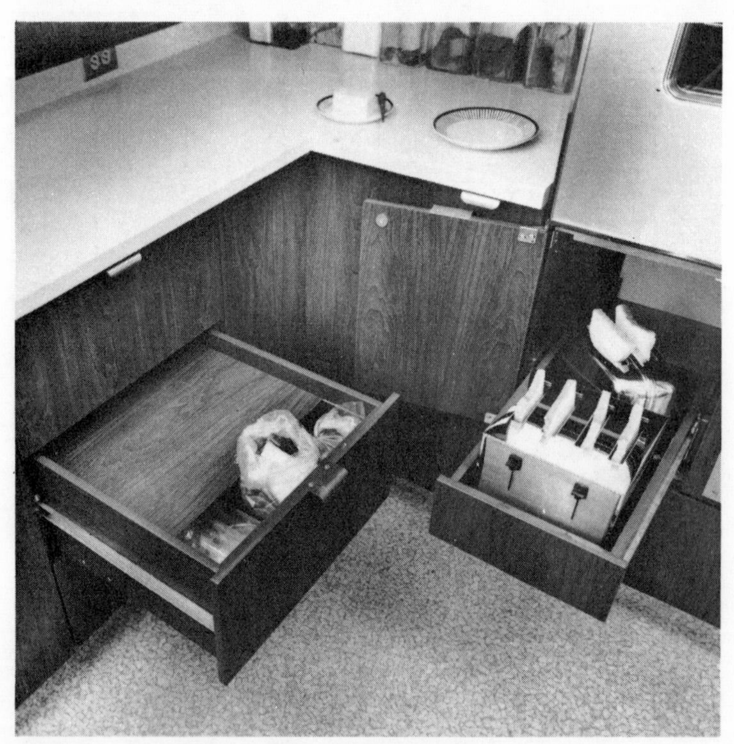

A CORNER FOR TOAST
Toasters are plugged in and left in glide-out drawers; outlet at rear. Metal-lined bread drawer is close by. Design: Ray Tischer.

CUPBOARD WITH TRIPLE OUTLET
Pull-out board, washable plastic shelf, triple outlet all combined. Archs.: Liddle & Jones.

For bulky appliances—a special hide-a-way

COUNTER-LEVEL STORAGE

Heavy and awkward to lift, electric mixer and meat grinder are stored at counter level behind doors that can be folded out of the way. Appliances plug into an outlet conveniently placed on the rear wall of the cupboard.

MIXER SWINGS DOWN

Mixer on platform swings down into cabinet when not in use. Design: Style Laminate Kitchens.

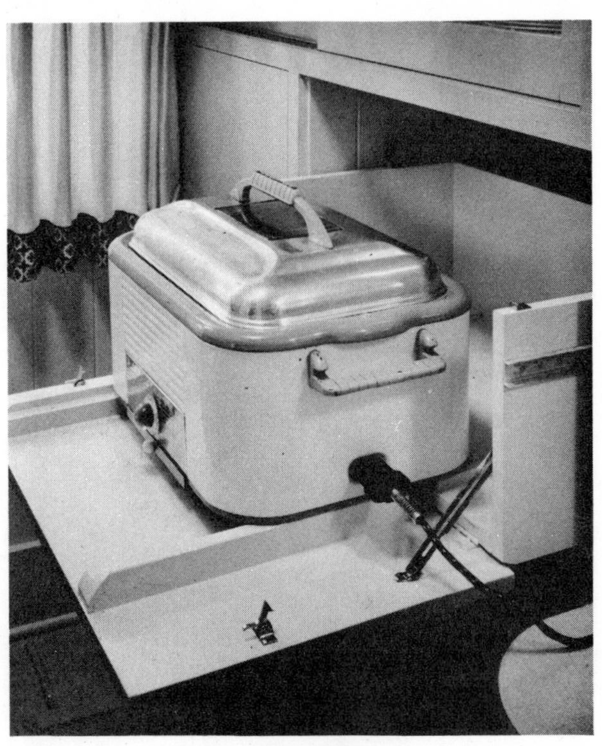

ROASTER SLIDES OUT

Cabinet that conceals this roaster rolls out, and roaster slides out on track on pull-down door; outlet nearby.

9 ways to store pots, pans

IN DEEP CUPBOARD
Pots and pans are stored in this deep cupboard without crowding. Lid rack on door. Arch.: Vladimir Ossipoff.

ABOVE THE RANGE
Area behind counter-top range has large panel with perforations sized for dowel pegs. Arch.: Richard N. Dennis.

IN LINED CUPBOARD
Perforated hardboard lines small closet. Archs.: Stedman & Williams.

ON HOOKS FROM SHELF
Pans hang on hooks from adjustable shelf. Archs.: Tucker & Shields.

ON PULL-OUT RODS
Pull-out rods and shelves store utensils. Archs.: Rushmore & Woodman.

IN LARGE DRAWERS

Large pan drawers pull out at point of use. Hanging utensils to right and left of range. Arch.: James G. Pulliam.

ON PULL-OUT SHELVES

Pots and pans are stored on pull-out shelves for easy access below counter-top range. Arch.: Keith R. Kolb.

IN A CUPBOARD WITHIN A CUPBOARD

This cupboard within a cupboard could be used anywhere. Grooved sides hold sliding trays for pan storage.

IN PARTITIONED DRAWER

Pan lids are stacked in partitioned drawer. Sides were grooved before assembling. Arch.: Arnold Gangnes.

Storage for sharp knives

PULL-OUT KNIFE RACK
Sharp knives are stored separately in this handy pull-out knife rack below cutting board. Arch.: Raymond Kappe.

KNIFE SLOT UNDER SHELF
A slot cut in shelf trim makes a simple knife holder. The shelf is 1/2-inch chipboard. Design: Harold Ogle.

SLOTS IN CHOPPING BLOCK
Knives, in slots in chopping block, are easy to reach. Design: Roscoe Wood.

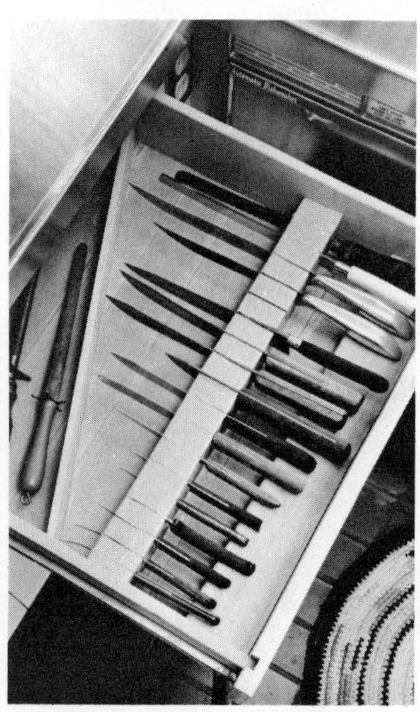

A COMPARTMENTED DRAWER
Knife handles are supported by block in drawer. Design: Cliff May.

MAGNETIC KNIFE STORAGE
Magnets from door catch hold knives in place. Design: David Tucker.

Convenient silver storage

SILVER STORED NEAR DISHWASHER
This silverware drawer is fitted into awkward corner space; has removable tray. Design: Janean.

DOUBLE DECKER STORAGE
Tray on counter fits in rear drawer and slides back or forth to reveal utensils below. Arch.: Alfred Preis.

CONVENIENT AND STABLE SILVER STORAGE
Silver chest is stored on a pull-out shelf (equipped with stops). Four 1/4-inch wood strips are nailed to shelf top to keep chest from sliding off; these fit snugly inside second set on bottom of chest. Design: Henry Lace.

Storage for

GLASSWARE, DINNERWARE

Elimination of breakage • Adjustable shelving • Stacking of dinnerware

Handling oversize pieces • Specialized storage wall • Visible storage units

Two-way storage for china, glasses • Practical and unusual ideas

Visible storage facilities are used by many families to display fine dinner pieces and glassware. For the "everyday" set, the kitchen cabinet still serves as the basic unit for storing. Consideration of accessibility and elimination of breakage are the most important factors for either set.

For your display pieces, installation of glass doors on cabinets can be decorative and also has the advantage of protecting against dust. Of course, open shelving can also be decorative. However, unless open shelves are out of the reach of careless hands, the display can become costly. If open shelving is best for your particular situation, set rims on the shelves and allow a one-inch safety space between stored items and the shelf edge.

Glassware

Everyday glassware—often made up of odd sizes, of broken sets, and of jelly and cheese glasses—is used at such a rapid rate that easy access overshadows any consideration for appearance. The uniformity of better glassware enables you to store a maximum number of pieces in a small area, but arranging the shelves to eliminate breakage can be tricky. Here are some suggestions for handling the features of all glassware:

Eliminate deep storage. This is a must to cut down on breakage. And it can be done simply by dividing the glasses between the front 6 inches of two shelves; this eliminates fumbling for that favorite glass which always seems to be behind 2 or 3 others. An alternate method is to install half-shelves against the back walls of the cabinets. In this way, flat dinnerware can be stored below the shelves and yet not interfere with the removal of the glasses.

Also, consider the possibilities of constructing a between-the-studs cabinet or reframing a cabinet that once held an ironing board. This type of cabinet will provide shelves which are about 4 inches deep—an adequate space for one-deep storage.

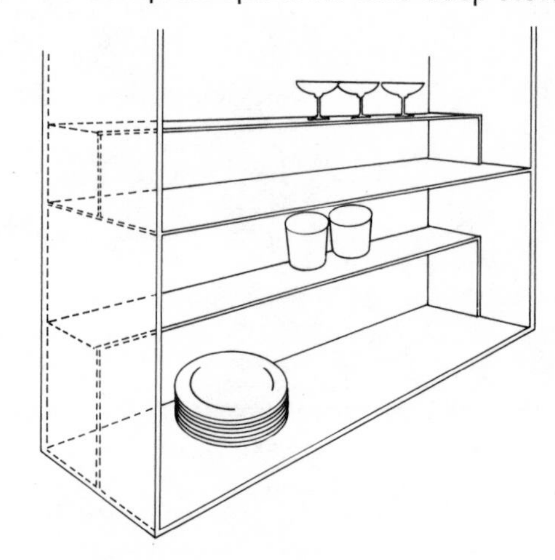

Half-shelves eliminate breakage

Make the shelves adjustable. This arrangement cuts waste space. One or two inches of space above the stored glasses is all that is required for easy removal. Adjustable shelves will fit the height of the glasses and also give you the finger space needed. You will find that several different sets of glasses can be stored in one shallow cabinet.

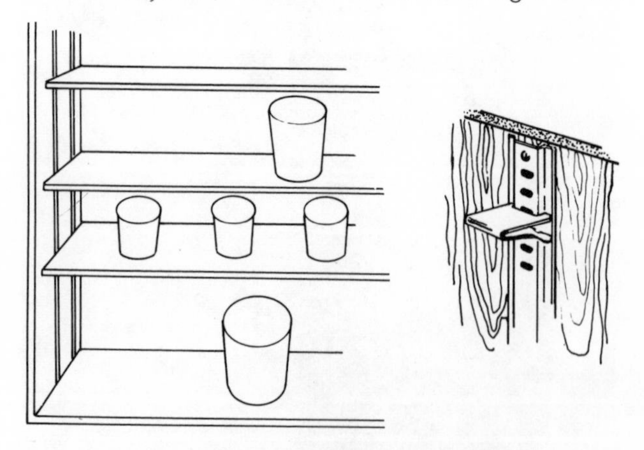

Adjustable shelves cut waste space

For dinnerware—stacking is good

One of the greatest sins generally associated with storage—stacking—can be done efficiently with dinnerware. Stacking of four, six, or eight pieces all the same size and shape not only saves space, but makes setting the table easier. Don't stack valuable pieces too high.

Uniformity is the key. The uniformity of dinnerware allows you to make the storage units the exact size of the items to be stored—that is, if you stack identical pieces. Limited on space? A shelf 12 inches deep will hold all your dinnerware—except for large platters and serving pieces.

Remember, if you store dinnerware only one deep, adjustment of shelves can be made to eliminate waste open space. But if you just don't have the space for one-deep storage, pull-out shelves could be the answer. Pull-out trays made of plastic or rubber and of varying sizes can easily be installed in most cabinets.

If you do have extra space and would like easy access to your dinnerware, vinyl-coated wire racks for vertical storage are available commercially.

How to handle oversize pieces. To store them flat, a shelf 16 inches deep is needed. A more popular way is to store these pieces on slanted shelves on a 12-inch base. By adjusting the degree of slant, platters up to 16 inches wide may be stored. Neither of these ideas will work for you? Then why not try leaning the larger pieces against the back wall of a cabinet? Although not as convenient as other methods, it may be the only answer if space is limited. A protecting strip of quarter-round molding is all that is needed to prevent sliding.

Don't stack the cups. Although the size of cups is fairly uniform, the shape is not. Stacking in this case is wrong, for several reasons: Appearance is messy; handles often protrude above the drinking level and the cups will not balance evenly; a handle can be broken or the rim be chipped while removing one cup; the temptation is to remove them by stacks, with droppage a likely result.

Again, one-deep storage can be the answer. Remember that if half-shelves work for glassware, then why not for cups? Or, you may prefer to hang your cups on special racks that slide out of the cabinet, or hooks mounted on the bottom of a cabinet shelf.

A single unit for most glassware and dinnerware

DINING ROOM BUFFET DESIGNED FOR DINNERWARE

This dining room buffet is designed to accommodate most types of dinnerware found in the home. Platters are stored in vertically-divided shelves; glassware and serving pieces above. Racks and shelves hold saucers, cups.

The compartments in this storage wall are specialized

FLOOR-TO-CEILING STORAGE WALL

Each section of storage wall in dining room opens independently, provides space for glasses, dinnerware, linens, less frequently used accessories. Tableware is placed on pull-out shelf while removing. Archs.: Benton & Park.

Two-way storage for china... glasses...

TWO-WAY STORAGE ABOVE PASS-THROUGH

Kitchen is separated from dining area without losing openness. Panel folds for counter. Arch.: Keith Kolb.

GLASSES REMOVED FROM EITHER SIDE

Glassware storage cabinet near dishwasher and sink separates kitchen from breakfast area. Arch.: Keith Kolb.

Visible storage units add color and design

CUPBOARD BETWEEN STUDS
Showcase for glassware is cupboard between 2x6 studs. Shelves are adjustable.

DISPLAY CASE ADDS COLOR AND DESIGN
Display case for collection of cups and saucers adds color and design to room. Shelves are grooved for saucers; glass doors slide.

Other storage ideas...practical and unusual...

SHALLOW CURVED SHELF
One-deep storage for cups on curved shelf; plates easy to remove.

SHELVES ARE VENTED
Air circulates through holes in shelf to dry glasses. Design: David Tucker.

VERTICAL DIVIDERS
Open rack is partitioned with plywood for storage of platters, trays.

Storage for

LINENS

Folding and sorting areas • How to prevent wrinkling

Pass-through cabinets • Shelving above washer and dryer

Adjustable shelving • Pull-out shelves

Two linen storage centers are required for most homes: one located in the kitchen, dining room, or family room for table linens, and the other in the bedroom wing or central hallway for bed and bath linens. Most homes are built with a central hallway storage unit. Therefore, the amount of extra storage needed for bed and bath linens usually depends on the size of your family and the amount of convenience you desire. Storage for table linens requires entirely different considerations.

Folding and sorting area

A major consideration for all linen storage is to provide for a folding and sorting area. If a counter top or table is not handy, it may be possible to build a drop-down or fold-out table in or near the storage closet. Although these units should be handy to the storage units, they should not interfere with the living area when not in use.

Table linen

The major problem in storing table linens is to prevent wrinkling. This can be difficult. Tablecloths and napkins tend to become wrinkled from their own weight and the shifting that comes when one linen is removed from the bottom of a stack. Of course, you can avoid heavy stacking—but will this do the job?

Adjustable shelving in existing closet or cabinet space not only cuts down on waste open space but allows you to store each linen set separately. You may even be able to add two or three extra shelves without altering the over-all dimensions of the storage unit. Delving down into a drawer for the favorite tablecloth and set of napkins is eliminated. Just enough hand room between the shelves to permit removal of linens is all that is required.

Pull-out shelves, although not adjustable, provide easier access to linens. Everything is visible and easy to reach when the shelf is pulled out; therefore, no extra space between shelves is needed. Replacement of freshly-ironed linens or removal for use is a simple task that will not disturb the other pieces.

Swing-out towel racks. These racks can be installed in a closet or an open section of a cabinet. Linens are easy to remove or replace on the movable arms.

A bin equipped with dowels. Made to fit available space, the bin can be equipped with dowels for storage of large table linens. Casters and drawer-pull handles will make it easy to remove the bin out into the open.

Cardboard tubing or cylinders. Obtainable from a fabric store, cardboard tubing permits you to roll your table linens, secure them with pins, and store the tubes in available space.

Bedding and bath towels

Wrinkling is usually not a problem with bed and bath linens. But for those bed linens that are sometimes ironed, the same principles used in storage of table linens can be used. How to store bed and bath linens near the bedroom area and the laundry center should be the concern. The solution to this problem really depends on the placement of the laundry. In many new homes, the laundry is located in the bedroom wing, near the center hallway storage unit. Still, additional storage space may be needed. If your laundry center is located in the utility area, then what is the solution? Here are two methods for solving either situation.

A pass-through cabinet is the best method for achieving a link with the bath and bedroom area—if the laundry is placed in the utility area. The linens

Pass-through cabinets save steps

can be sorted, folded, and stored as they come from the dryer. As they are needed, each piece can be removed through the opposite side of the closet. Many pass-through units include clothes bins which can be opened in the bedroom or bath for loading and then be emptied in the laundry.

Shelves above the washer and dryer can serve as additional storage space—if the laundry is placed

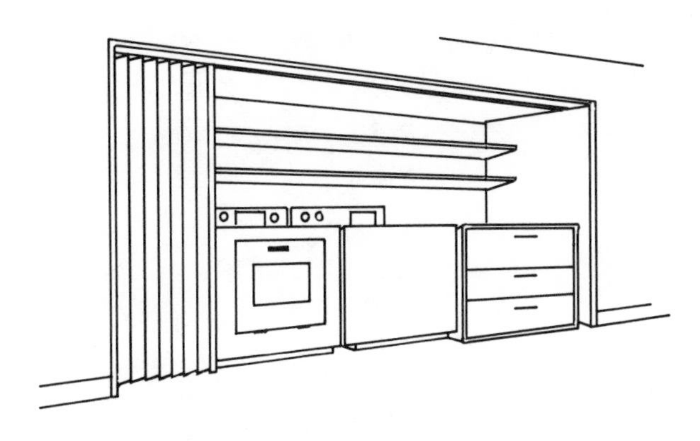

Extra storage space around appliances

in the bedroom wing. There may also be space beside the appliances for clothes bins or drawers for storage of laundry and cleaning supplies.

(For further ideas on obtaining extra storage space in the bedroom wing, see the chapter on storage of bathroom supplies.)

Pull-out shelves and drawers provide easy access

LINENS VISIBLE AT A GLANCE
Open-faced drawers slide out for easy access to table linens. Arch.: Roy Wilson.

BELOW SERVING COUNTER
Pull-out drawers of built-in dining room storage cabinet store table linens conveniently close to dining table. Design: Roy Krell.

Narrow shelving is good

NARROW DRAWERS PREVENT STACKING
Large cut-outs on drawer pulls make linens visible at a glance; narrow depth prevents heavy stacking, wrinkles.

DRAWERS GRADUATE IN SIZE
Built-in cabinet stores linens in graduating drawers. Napkins are in upper drawers; larger linens below.

Hang linens, avoid wrinkles

ON SWING-OUT TOWEL RACKS
Swing-out towel racks keep stored table linens relatively unwrinkled. Movable arms make linens easy to remove.

IN PLYWOOD BIN WITH DOWELS
Equipped with drawer-pull handles, plywood bin with dowels rolls out on casters. Design: Junius Driggs.

Bedding can also be hung

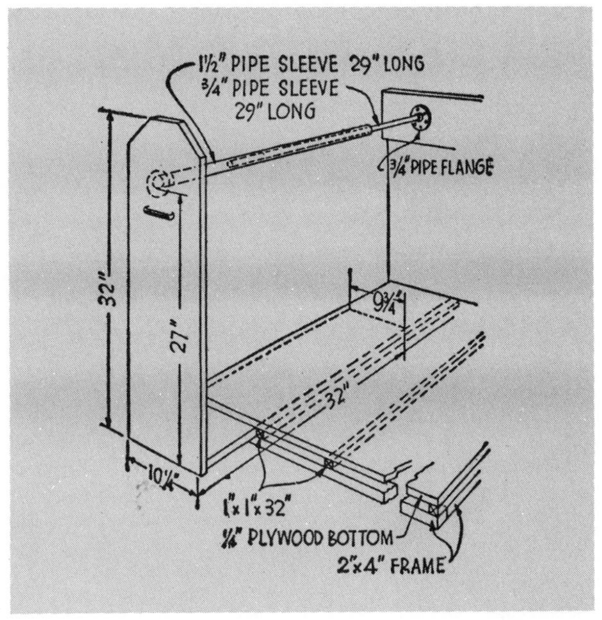

VENTED BLANKET STORAGE

Vented blanket "stows" give airiness to storage cabinet. Stows slide on waxed floor of cabinet. Bath towels and other flat pieces are stored on wide shelving above pullouts. Shelves are lightly stacked for easy removal.

Pass-throughs save steps

CLOSET LEADS TO LAUNDRY ROOM

From laundry side you see doors that conceal closet. Drop-down counter for folding. Design: Jan Currey.

HALLWAY CONNECTED TO UTILITY ROOM

Linens used most often are stored at eye level; seldom-used pieces fit on top, bottom. Design: Louis Shafer.

Storage for

BATHROOM SUPPLIES

Replacing old cabinets • Adding cabinets without remodeling

Floor-to-ceiling cabinets • Space savers and conveniences • Towel ladder

Pole shelves • Retractable steps for children

How much bathroom storage you need depends on the amount of storage in other rooms. For example if your hall closet is adequate for storing linens and cleaning supplies are stored in a central cleaning closet, then a medicine cabinet and perhaps a clothes hamper or bin will meet your needs. But, what if you find yourself face to face with relieving overcrowded conditions in other parts of the house?

Extensive remodeling not a "must"

If you are going to remodel a bathroom, it is only common sense to consider including some built-in storage space. But there are several possibilities for adding cabinets and closets in the bathroom without remodeling and without interfering with your floor space.

Replace old cabinets with modern commercial units designed to hang on a wall or fit between the studs. Often, two or three cabinets hung to fill a wall will accommodate all the tubes, jars, and bottles that collect on counters and window sills.

A hint to remember if you decide to build your own cabinet: Set the shelves 4 to 6 inches apart, with at least one shelf 9 inches high to accommodate taller bottles.

Enclose a section of open wall. Cabinets need be only 8 to 10 inches deep to hold linens and cleaning supplies. If they are fitted between the studs, they will project into the room only 4 to 6 inches.

Enclose space beneath the wash basin. A free-standing cabinet can simply be a bin (with a slot cut in the back to allow for the drain pipe), or shelving can be attached to the cabinet sides and on the doors. Remember to leave some working room in case the plumbing needs repair.

Add space savers and conveniences. Many commercial items are available, most of which are quite easy to install. One such item is a towel ladder. Reaching from floor to ceiling or from vanity to ceiling, this convenience can have as many rungs as you like—if you construct it to fit the bathroom. It allows you to display your prettiest towels and have them easily accessible. Another space saver is a pole shelf. Placed against a wall or placed to take advantage of free wall space above the toilet, these units have interchangeable and adjustable shelves. Other items include a two-roll paper holder which fits into a 10⁵/₈" x 5¹/₈" wall opening, dispensers for facial tissues which can be attached to the wall, and a toothbrush, tumbler and soap rack which revolves into a recess in the wall.

If you have small children, the bottom drawer of your vanity cabinet can be fitted with a solid top and used as a retractable step for reaching the wash bowl.

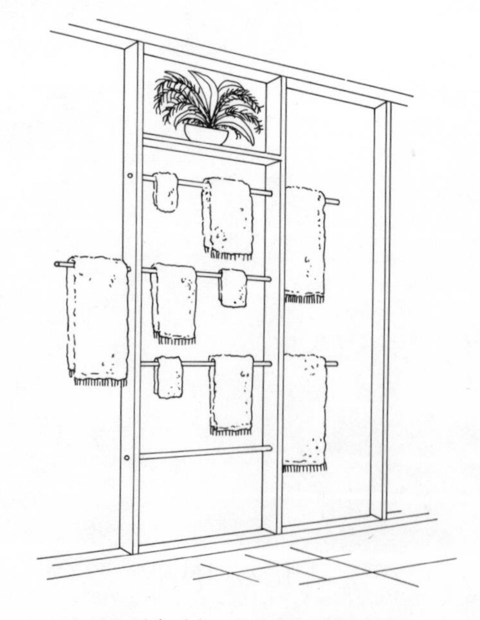

A towel ladder can be colorful

Floor-to-ceiling cabinets for linens, medicinal supplies

PARTITION-DEEP CABINETS
Between-the-studs space used for storage cabinet. Towel hangers are door pulls. Arch.: Anne Rysdale.

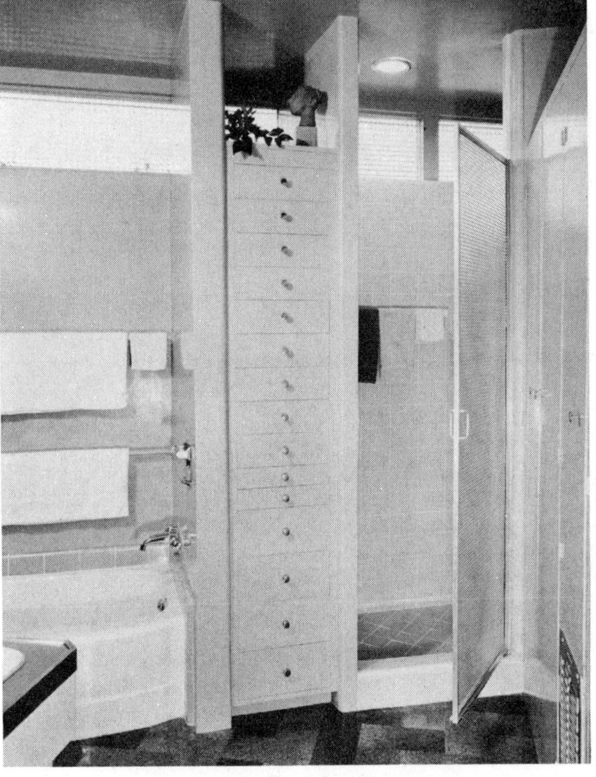

DRAWERS IN VARYING HEIGHTS
Partition between shower and tub is series of drawers in varying heights for linens. Arch.: Lloyd Ruocco.

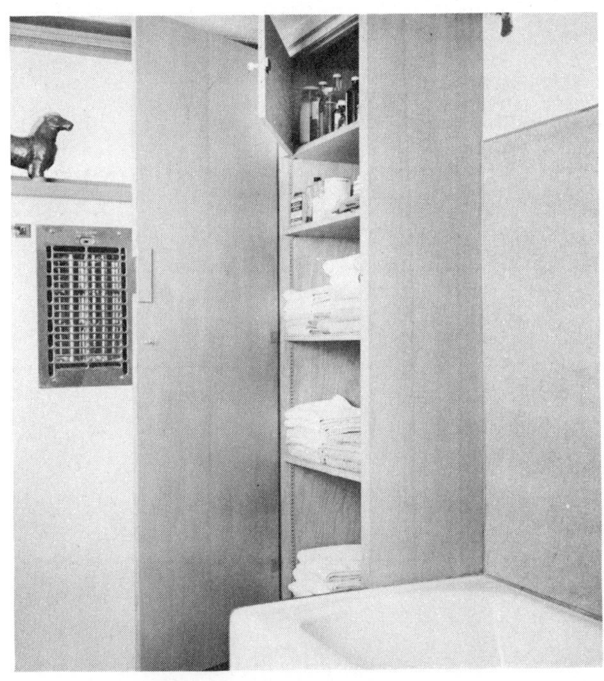

CLOSET WITH ADJUSTABLE SHELVES
Floor-to-ceiling cabinet is handy for storing linens; poisons on high shelf, can be locked. Arch.: Ellis Jacobs.

OVERSIZE MEDICINE CABINET
Robe closet and large clothes hamper are combined with medicine cabinet. Design: Marge Oppenheimer.

Bathroom hide-a-ways

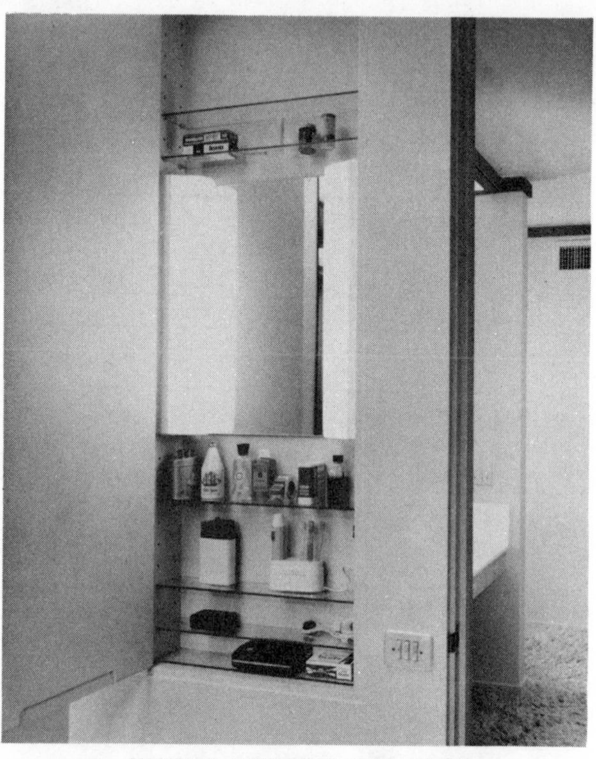

SHAVING CABINET TUCKED AWAY
Tucked into an unused corner, shaving cabinet has mirror, ample shelves, electric outlet. Archs.: Benton & Park.

PEG BOARD PANEL CONCEALS SHELVES
Hidden shelves above tub store towels, washcloths; open shelves hold miscellany. Arch.: Vladimir Ossipoff.

SMALL CABINET ATTACHED TO WALL
Unit is attached to wall by screws through fibreboard. Glass doors provide mirror area. Arch.: George Andrews.

HANDY STORAGE OF TOILETRIES
Planter at end of tub adds decorative touch and storage space for toiletries, cosmetics. Design: J. R. Davidson.

ADDITIONAL SHELVES AND TOWEL RACK

Without changes in walls or fixtures, this bathroom gets a new look and more storage space by the addition of a floor-to-ceiling towel rack, shelves. Framework of both units is made from 1 by 8 fir. Design: Mrs. John Patterson.

UNUSUAL PANEL COVERS SMALL CABINET

Pieces of rosewood in varying sizes are glued on plywood panel that covers cabinet. Design: John Kapel.

PARTITIONED DRAWERS

Interior of drawer in bathroom vanity is partitioned with 1/4-inch plywood. Archs.: Beal, Bidwell, & Macky.

Storage for

LAUNDRY, CLEANING SUPPLIES

Choice of laundry locations • Conveniences for simplifying laundering chores

Laundry sorter • Drip-dry areas • Mending center

Storage for ironing paraphernalia • Designing a central cleaning closet

In "olden days" when washing meant tubs and washboards and clotheslines and sheer back-breaking labor, there was little choice as to where you put the laundry. It had to go in the utility room next to the back porch, or in the basement. Today, although most housewives prefer to have a separate utility room, most medium-sized homes just don't have the necessary square footage. What do you do if this is the case in your home? Fortunately, the washer and dryer can go anywhere in the house if you can provide them with the proper wiring and plumbing.

What location is right for you?

Wherever the laundry is placed, it can be to your advantage to have additional space around the washer and dryer to allow for other items that help to make the laundry process run smoothly. For example:

. . . a sink for scrubbing grease and stains
. . . storage shelves for soaps and bleaches
. . . a place for an ironing board and iron

The garage offers advantages of a separate utility room — and is often chosen first for economy: economy in cost of plumbing as you frequently can tie into the existing kitchen plumbing system, economy in not having to give the area a finished look, and economy in using the extra space often provided in a garage. Besides economy, other advantages are accessibility for repairs and easy cleanup if overflow should occur.

On the other hand, this location is not generally convenient to the source of dirty clothes. Also, the garage can be frequently cold and drafty—or it can be overly warm.

A hallway in the bedroom wing is often chosen as the laundry center because of the proximity to the largest source of soiled clothes and linens. Here the linens can be washed, dried, folded, and returned directly to closets and drawers. Families with small children (lots of laundry, little ironing) find this location especially convenient. Also, plumbing is no problem. The equipment can usually be connected to the bathroom plumbing.

However, it isn't always easy to work laundry in with the other activities in this area. Noise may be a problem, venting for heat and moisture may be difficult, and accumulation of odors from bleaches and other cleaning agents may be objectionable. And possible overflow of water could make this location a costly choice.

The kitchen is one of the most logical choices. Here you can do the laundry at the same time other household tasks are performed. Plumbing facilities are available. The dryer can usually be vented to an outside wall. Laundry can be an actual part of the kitchen or a screened extension. However, there may be some objection to the added noise and clutter. Since the kitchen is a busy enough place *without* added activity, you may prefer the family room or the lanai. In either of the latter locations, folding panel doors can close off the laundry center when not in use.

Making your day shorter

Here are several ideas that may be useful in planning improvements and simplifying laundering chores:

A special place for drip-drys. This eliminates the line over the bathtub or shower. Because a drip-dry area requires a drain, it's usually best to provide for this area when you build or remodel.

A small mending center. Pull-out trays take hardly any space and you can mend clothes as they come from the dryer.

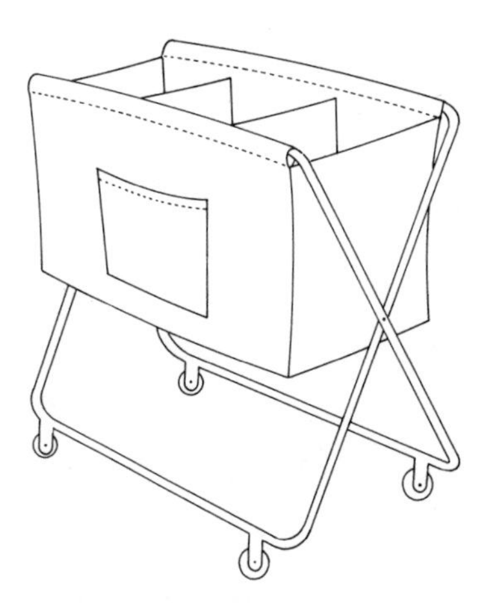

A laundry sorter makes work easier

A laundry sorter. This simple innovation for collecting clothes from the bedroom area can do a great deal in helping to make your work easier.

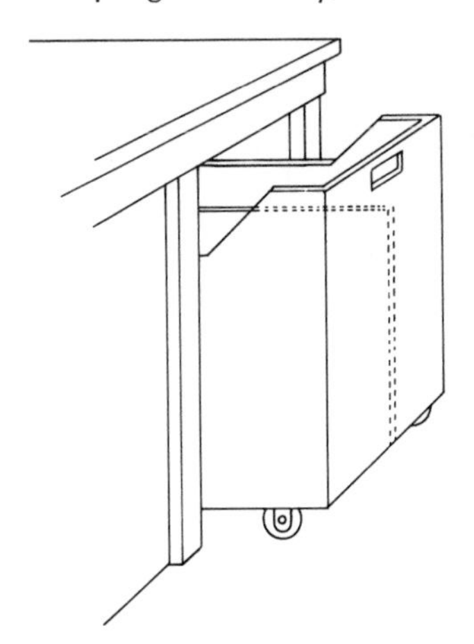

Handy bins for sorting clothes

Roll-around bins and drop-down bins. These are handy for sorting clothes and can be built into a small cabinet.

Simple touches. Arrangements that make good sense include a hand towel or a roll of paper towels hung beside the laundry tray, and adjustable shelves in the surrounding cabinets.

All cleaning items in one place

A single storage closet for all cleaning implements is intended to save time and trouble in the daily process of keeping the house in order. Rather than having to dig a mop out of a closet in the utility room and then search for a pail and soap under the kitchen sink, it is handier to have all cleaning items in one place. *Exceptions:* Cleaning supplies used only in the kitchen belong in the cabinet under the sink. Cleaning implements for the bathroom belong in the bathroom.

How to design a central closet. The wide range of shapes and sizes of cleaning items to be stored—brooms, mops, vacuum cleaner, waxer, dust mops, dust pans, window washing equipment, waxes, soaps, disinfectants, buckets—points up the difficulty of designing a single closet for these implements. There are prefabricated metal units available which provide adequate storage for most homes. However, if you would like to adapt a spare closet or an empty wall space to fit your household needs, here are a few suggestions to follow:

. . . for depth, 16 to 20 inches is adequate
. . . width can be variable, but 24 inches is a good minimum
. . . height should be at least 65 inches
. . . hang implements on back wall
. . . use back of door for long attachments
. . . install shelves on side wall for small items

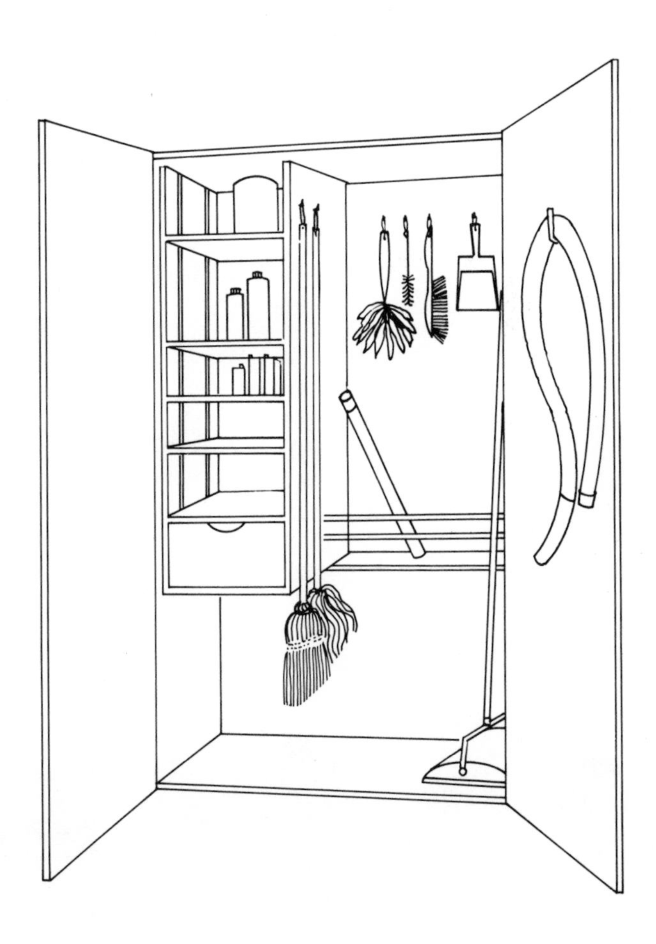

All cleaning items in one place

What corner in your house has room for the laundry?

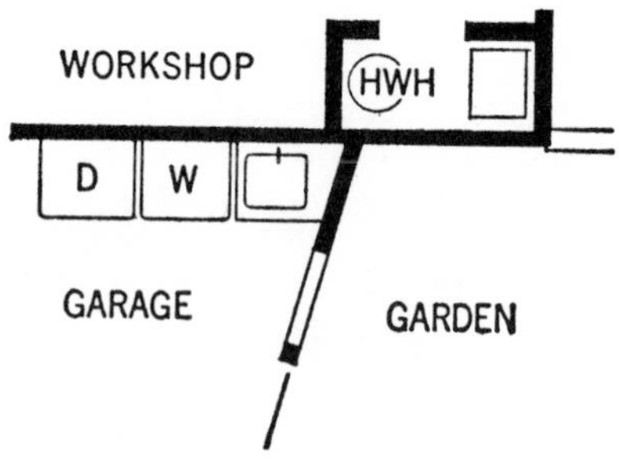

IN CORNER OF GARAGE
Window from another part of house makes corner of the garage a light, airy laundry location. Black units, when not in use are covered with bright orange sailcloth. Clothes are in wicker basket. Note sink and cabinet. Design: Norman Manoogian.

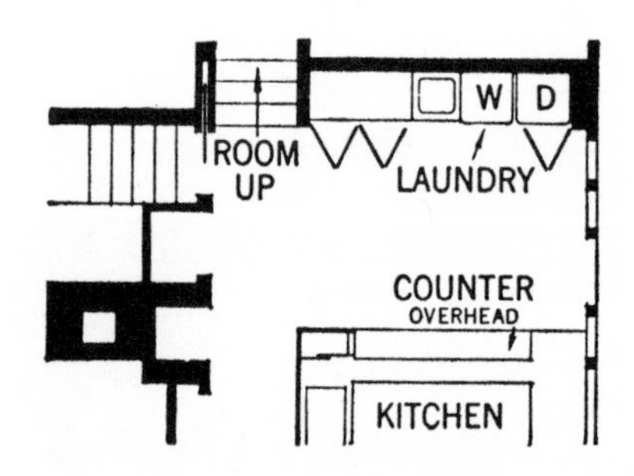

AN ALCOVE IN KITCHEN
This laundry is part of kitchen, yet is separated from it by folding doors. Alcove has sink, clothesline, shelves for soaps and cleaning supplies, and exhaust fan. Note small container at end of clothesline for clothespins. Arch.: Herman Brookman.

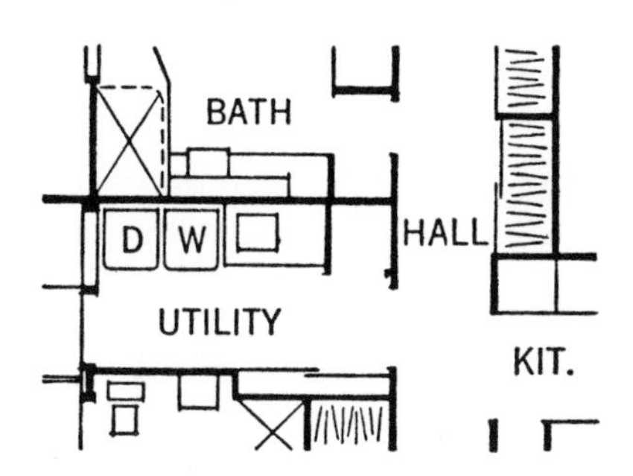

SEPARATE UTILITY ROOM
Utility room is located in bedroom wing, across hall from kitchen. Door opens to drying yard and garden. Equipment is connected to bathroom plumbing. Room includes closet for ironing equipment and sink. Archs.: Whitaker and Slavsky.

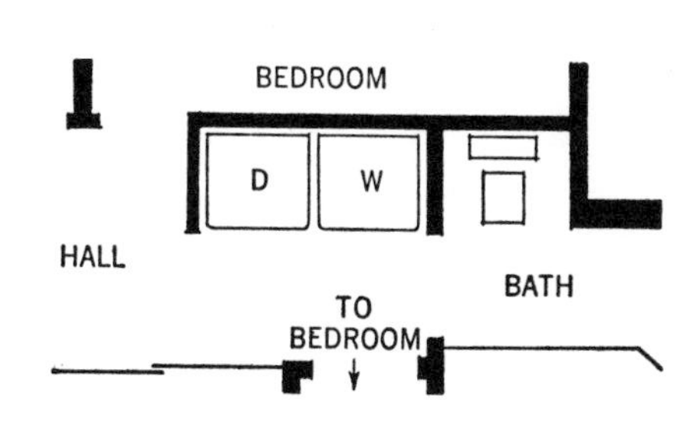

IN BEDROOM HALL
Families with small children and much laundry requiring little ironing find bedroom hall an ideal location for laundry equipment. This area is skylit by day. Large closet across hall stores supplies. Machine tops form counter for sorting and folding.

Here are some other locations for the laundry

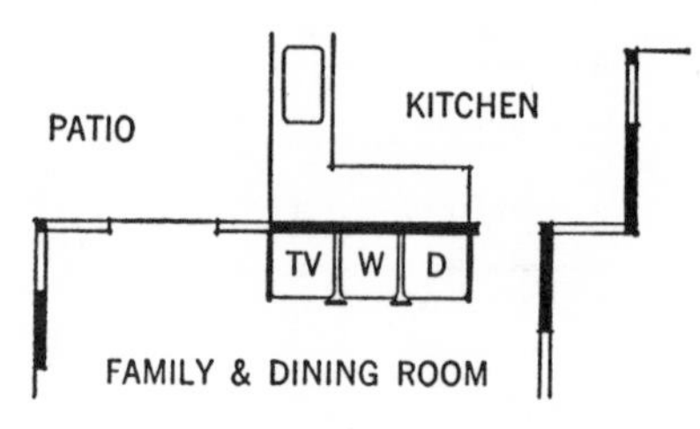

IN FAMILY ROOM

Mahogany plywood cabinet houses washer and dryer in family-and-dining room. Appliances are piped in with equipment in kitchen, through door at right. Upper section is wall hung; lower part pulls out from wall. Design: W. Verne Stevenson.

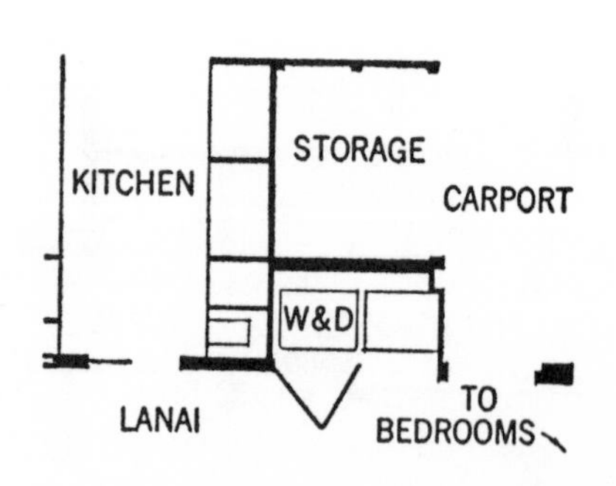

IN LANAI

Laundry on this lanai is in ideal central location. Closet has washer-dryer, roll-out bins, counter space for sorting, storage shelves. Dryer is vented through storage room in carport. Storage area is covered with folding doors. Arch.: Alfred Preis.

Conveniences to help simplify laundering routine

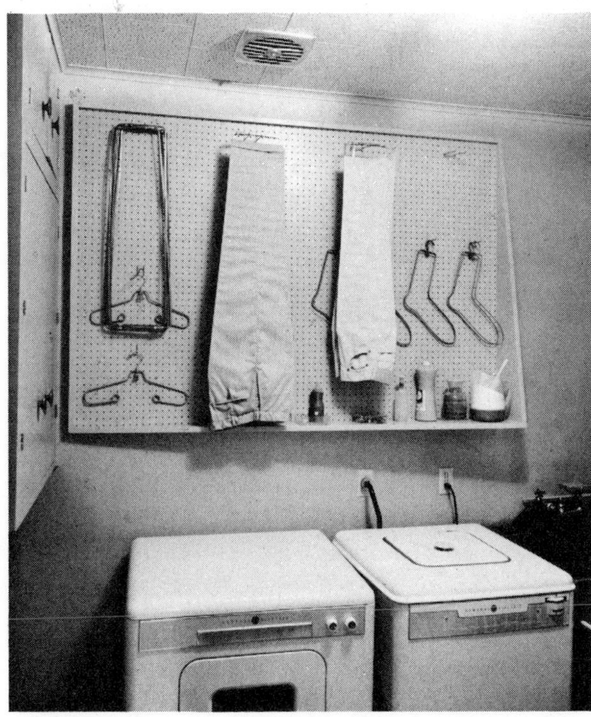

PERFORATED HARDBOARD PANEL
Right and bottom sections of frame slant from depth of 1 inch to 8 inches at lower right corner making shelf.

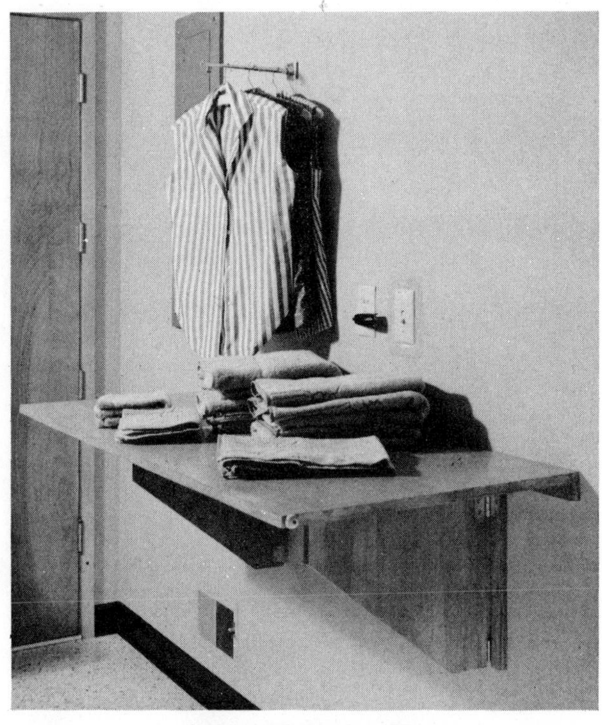

FLIP-UP SORTING TABLE
Flip-up sorting table in laundry room also doubles as place to put dishes and glasses. Design: S. C. Robinson.

PULL-OUT IRONING BOARD
Full-size ironing board and roll-out bin in kitchen are handy for laundering chores. Arch.: William J. Bain, Jr.

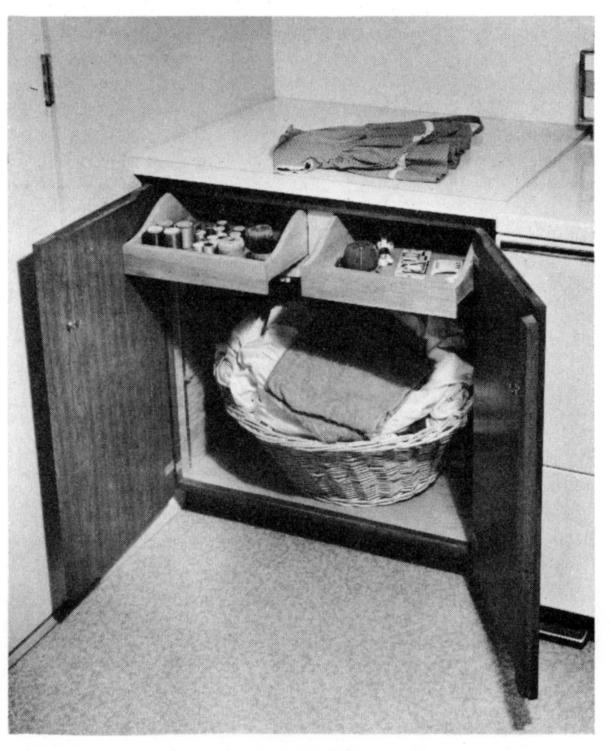

DRAWERS FOR MENDING SUPPLIES
Two pull-out trays in small counter-height cabinet hold materials for quick mending jobs. Archs.: Allan & Olsson.

How to store the paraphernalia for ironing

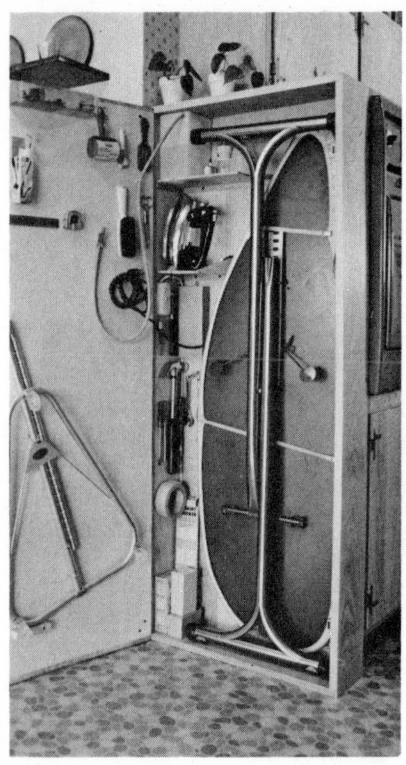

SHALLOW CLOSET CONCEALS IRONING EQUIPMENT

Closed, ironing storage closet presents a neat façade, flush with adjoining wall and fronting floor space away from kitchen traffic. Open, closet reveals iron, board, mending supplies. Design: G. Howard Burch.

IRONING BOARD FOLDS AGAINST DOOR

When not in use, ironing board folds conveniently into its own storage space. Design: L. Harold Whitaker.

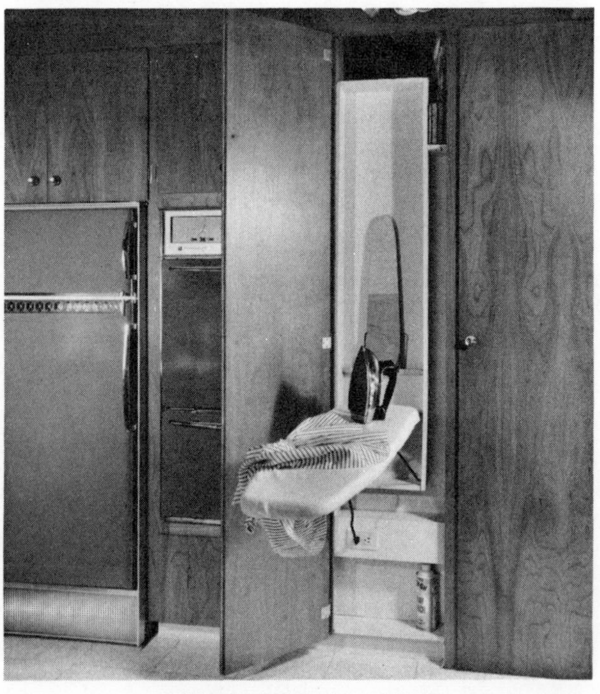

BUILT-IN IRONING BOARD

Wall at open end of U-shaped kitchen includes built-in ironing board; outlet below. Design: Dallas E. Zeiger.

A single closet for all cleaning implements and supplies

CLEANING EQUIPMENT GOES BETWEEN LEVELS
Many steps are saved with this cleaning closet located beside the stairway landing in two-story house. Closet has folding doors. Design: Halsey Jones.

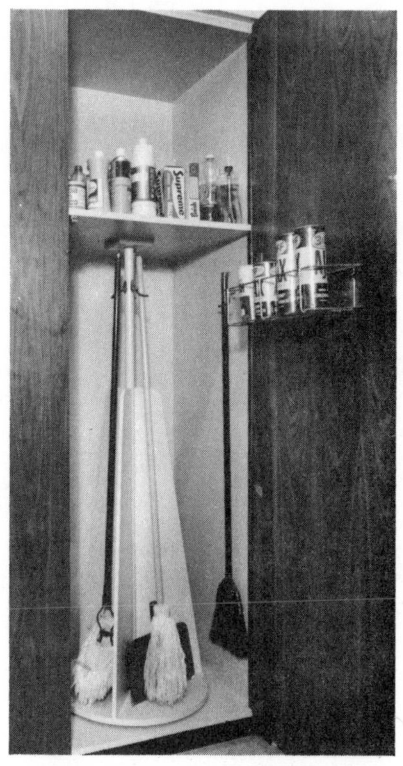

REVOLVING BROOM STORAGE
Revolving stand uses small space in closet. Design: Fred Blair Green.

COMBINATION CLEANING CLOSET
Cleaning implements and supplies share closet with ironing board and iron. Design: Norman V. Manoogian.

ADJUSTABLE SHELVES HOLD ACCESSORIES
Cleaning closet has hooks on walls for dust mops, brushes; rests on shelf. Adjustable shelves hold accessories.

Storage for

SEWING EQUIPMENT

Combination work-storage center • A free-standing sewing center

Closet-sized workrooms • Housing a standard model machine

Organizing space around machine

The enthusiastic and creative home seamstress desires efficient storage—with all objects within easy reach—as much as any other home hobbyist. And she is often inspired to create efficient storage by the need to keep her sewing equipment away from busy and curious little hands.

Everything within easy reach

When you purchased your sewing machine, you may also have purchased a combination table-cabinet. If so, your storage problems are solved. If not, you probably have need for a combination work-storage center. Not much space is needed.

A combination work-storage center

A closet-sized area can hold a sewing center. In fact, a space the size of a narrow bookcase can be adequate—if you plan your storage and counter space carefully.

Housing a standard model machine requires a space approximately 20 inches deep, 35 inches wide, and 36 inches high. A portable requires equal depth, but only 25 inches of width and 16 inches of height. You have just the place with these dimensions? This is good if you simply want to store your machine when not in use. But if you plan on this area to also be your working area, a few extra inches of space behind the machine are needed to accommodate material as it is passing through.

Mount your machine on a swing-out shelf, a movable cart, or a sliding platform. This may be the only solution to finding enough working space, storing it out of sight, and not having to lift or carry the bulky appliance when it is needed.

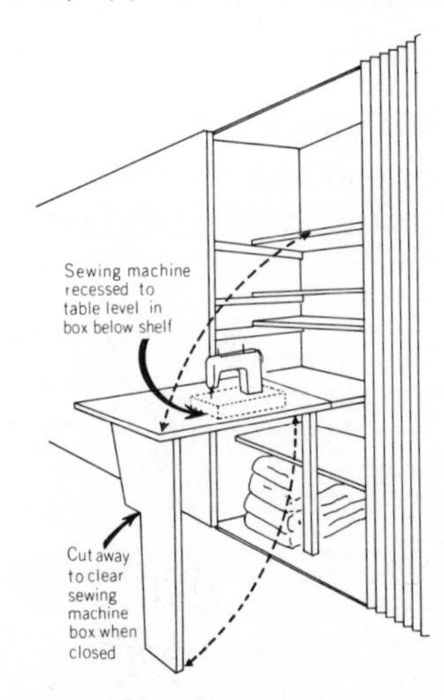

Sewing counter is designed to fold up

Keep things within easy reach. Organizing the space around your machine to achieve this is not always easy to do. However, you can strive for the best arrangement keeping these points in mind:

Pull-out shelves, shallow drawers, and narrow shelving are best for storing pointed instruments, and they eliminate probing in deep drawers.

Partitioning drawers according to the items to be stored avoids entanglements and facilitates replacement of objects.

Pull-out shelves can also be partitioned and fitted with small edgings that will keep items from falling.

Drawers can be partitioned to the exact width of spools of thread, or the spools can be mounted on dowels or rails set in a wall on the back of a door.

Commercially made spool and bobbin holders could be the simple answer to keeping small items within easy reach. These plastic containers fit easily into a drawer; also they are sturdy enough to remain as a storage unit on top of a counter.

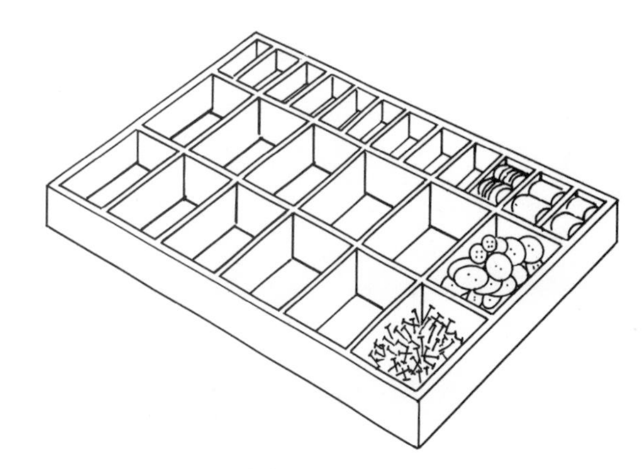

Partitioned drawers for small items

If you like to sew—a combination work-storage center

SEWING MACHINE CAN BE SET UP QUICKLY

Utility room is daylit by generous-sized skylight. Sewing machine can be set up near the washer, dryer. Counter doubles as extra table for lunch when kitchen eating counter is crowded. Archs.: Rushmore and Woodman.

This sewing center is designed to be free-standing

FOLD-DOWN LEAF BECOMES WORKING TABLE

Sewing cabinet is designed to be free-standing, movable, and presentable. In open position, fold-down leaf is work table for patterns, and platform to hold material coming out of machine. Design: Mrs. Frank Haines.

IN CLOSED POSITION

Cabinet stands out about 18 inches from wall, fits in with other furniture.

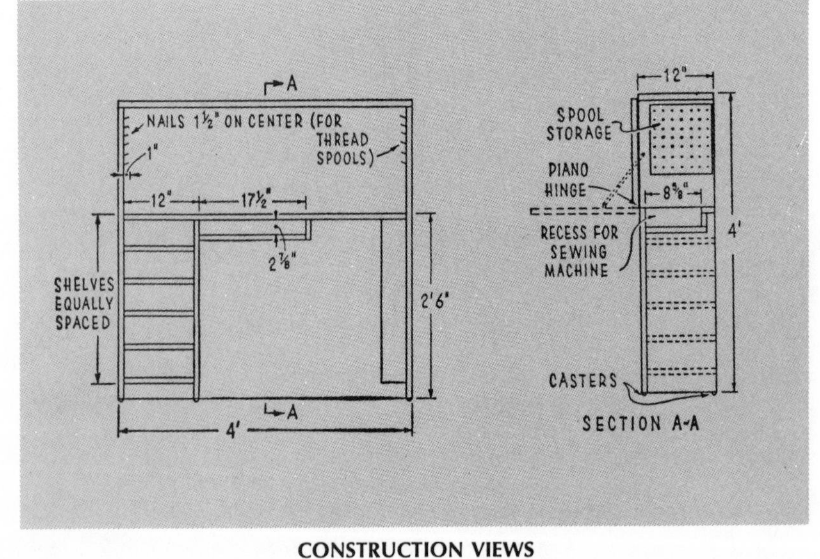

CONSTRUCTION VIEWS

Rear construction view (left) shows dimensions and placement of cabinet, shelves. Section view (right) shows how shelves, fold-down flap are attached.

A closet-sized area can hold a workroom

MATERIALS CLOSE AT HAND
Table swings down, materials are close by. Arch.: Donald Goldman.

BUILT-IN COUNTER
Alcove has built-in counter, drawers, cabinets. Arch.: William L. Fletcher.

STAND-UP HEIGHT COUNTER
Ironing board stored under counter without folding. Arch.: Ted Bower.

Other ideas if you are really limited on space

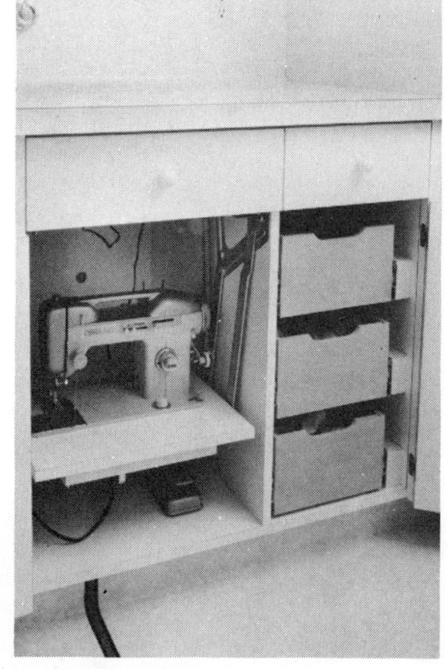

MACHINE SWINGS DOWN AND UNDER
Mounted on a laminated plastic shelf, sewing machine is raised by same type of hardware used to raise mixers. Outlet at rear. Design: Harry Ferguson.

SEWING EQUIPMENT HANGS
Equipment board is 28 by 30 inches. Design: Mrs. William Montgomery.

Storage for

CLOTHING

A walk-in closet • The storage wall • Planning closet space

Separate dressing centers • Shallow units for folded garments

Storage for handbags and shoes • Open shelving for hats and accessories

Storage for jewelry • Closets for chore or outdoor garments

The three general areas for clothes storage are the bedroom or dressing area, the hall closet, and the chore closet. Does your family require all three? Some families prefer to combine clothes storage with other general storage facilities in a room divider or storage wall. This preference often eliminates the hall or chore closet. Whatever your needs, clothing storage in the bedroom or dressing area usually requires the most consideration with the latter two requiring the least.

Smaller bedrooms—detailed storage planning

The bedroom with surplus closet space is a rarity. Bedrooms aren't as large as they were in the houses of yesteryear (with the possible exception of the master bedroom). Consequently, the need for detailed planning for storage space in the bedroom has been amplified.

The storage units required in a bedroom or dressing area are: rods for hanging garments; drawers for folded clothes; specialized shelving for hats, purses, gloves, and other accessories; and a rack or special closet for shoes. It used to be that these storage units were separated—a wardrobe closet, one or two chests of drawers, a dressing table. But to save space and coordinate clothes storage, architects generally combine all units into one—either a walk-in closet or a storage wall.

Design storage wall for individual needs

The walk-in closet may be just the arrangement you need, if you can afford its space requirements when planning a new home. Otherwise, be prepared to do extensive remodeling, possibly necessitating professional help. Whichever unit you choose, you will be rewarded with ample space for clothes rods on two walls and plenty of drawers and shelving, plus room for easy access.

The storage wall—a floor-to-ceiling unit—usually covers or forms one entire wall of the room. The standard depth requirement for this unit is only 24 inches. If you don't have quite that much space, installation of a pull-out clothes rod that has clothes hung parallel to the door might be your answer. The clothes rod is pulled into the room while you select garments—then returned to the closet when not in use. These easy-to-install metal rods are available to fit any size closet.

Many home builders conserve on space and materials by making one storage wall serve two rooms. These units may or may not be non-supporting partitions. A wall of this type can be approximately 36 inches deep, with 24 inches on one side being used for the wardrobe, and 12 inches on the other side being used for bookcases and shoes.

When planning your storage wall, keep in mind that there is no "standard" organization. The interior can be designed to meet your individual needs. Of course, you will want to put every available inch of space to work. Here are some suggestions to help you when planning your storage unit:

Provide easy access. Sliding, swinging, folding, or full-access doors all provide easy access to a unit of this type. The choice of any one will eliminate unusable corners and will enable you to reach every item stored. If swinging doors are used, extra storage space can be gained by installing shelves, rods, hooks, and other accessories on the inside surface for storing small items.

Group garments of equal size. When planning space for clothes, group them according to length. This will provide uniform space beneath hung clothes to accommodate another clothes rod or space for drawers or shelves.

Use shallow units for folded garments. Folded garments may be handled in one of many ways. The basic consideration is to have them stored in shallow units to avoid heavy piling and wrinkling. Drawers and sliding shelves are the most practical for achieving this. A 12-inch depth should be adequate, but depth and width of these units depend primarily on how you fold the garments.

Small area can store many shoes. Because of their uniformity in size, shoes give you an opportunity to store a number of pairs in a small area. If you can devote a very narrow (10 or 12-inch) opening, 4 to 6 feet high and 12 inches deep, you can store 6 to 8 pairs of shoes by using adjustable shelving. Actually, you can make shoes fit into any space available. A narrow opening between studs is deep enough for a hanging shoe bag; slanted floor of a closet can accommodate several pairs; a rolling cart that slides under hanging clothes can keep shoes in tidy order; commercially-built racks inserted under hanging clothes keep shoes off the floor and easy to reach.

Use open shelving for hats and accessories. Hats, purses, gloves, and jewelry can be stored within easy reach by compartmenting an open section of wall in 12-inch squares. Seldom-used articles may be stored in shelves above hanging clothes or in the lowest drawer in a chest.

Hall closet serves double purpose

A hall closet usually serves a double purpose by storing the coats, hats, and umbrellas of your family and providing temporary storage for the wraps of guests.

The hall closet can serve as a screen between the front door and living areas. It can also be combined with a desk, music cabinets, or bookcase to form a complete free-standing storage wall.

Basic requirements are simple. This unit should be at least 24 inches deep and 24 inches wide. The clothes pole should be high enough to handle long coats. It should also have a shelf hung approximately 3 inches above the clothes rod for hats and accessories and a space for overshoes.

Chore closet can be all-purpose

A closet for storing chore clothes and outdoor garments might be just what you need. Of course, it depends on just how many times you have rummaged through the bedroom closet or other nooks and crannies searching for that faded pair of jeans to wear while painting—or a raincoat for that unexpected shower—or the pair of shoes to wear while working in the garden. Here are some suggestions for making this closet a convenient storage space:

Hang garments on hooks. Because there is really no need to keep chore clothes neat and tidy, they may be hung on hooks rather than hangers. This reduces space needed. A space 16 to 20 inches deep, 4 feet wide, and 6 feet high will do the trick. However, if there are coats or shirts you want on hangers, place the hangers on the clothes hooks so the width of the piece of clothing is parallel to the door. The hooks should be placed at least 60 inches off the floor and 10 inches apart. If you

A closet for chore and outdoor garments

decide to set a shelf above the hooks, leave 3 to 4 inches of clearance space below the shelf to facilitate hanging garments on hooks.

Shoes may be stored on the floor or on a shelf. If the shoes need to dry out, a lath shelf about 4 inches off the floor will provide air circulation. To facilitate easy cleaning, the shelf can be set on cleats—not nailed down.

Combination closets for husband and wife

CLOSET WALL SERVES TWO PEOPLE

Waste space is held to minimum by close calculation of garment lengths in wardrobe section. Sliding doors are removed for photo; 2-foot recess between doors and storage gives entry space. Arch.: Harold Gangnes.

ON WIFE'S SIDE

Shoes are stored in pull-out cabinets; every pair is accessible, yet out of sight when cabinet is closed.

ON MAN'S SIDE

Large cabinet has rack for shoes. Sweaters, other folded pieces are on pull-out trays. Tie rack in wall recess.

DRESSING CENTERS BACK TO BACK

Her dressing center has more shelves, drawers, upper and lower bar for blouses, skirts. Longer garments hang elsewhere. His closet is concealed by folding door that activates light switch. Arch.: Morgan Stedman.

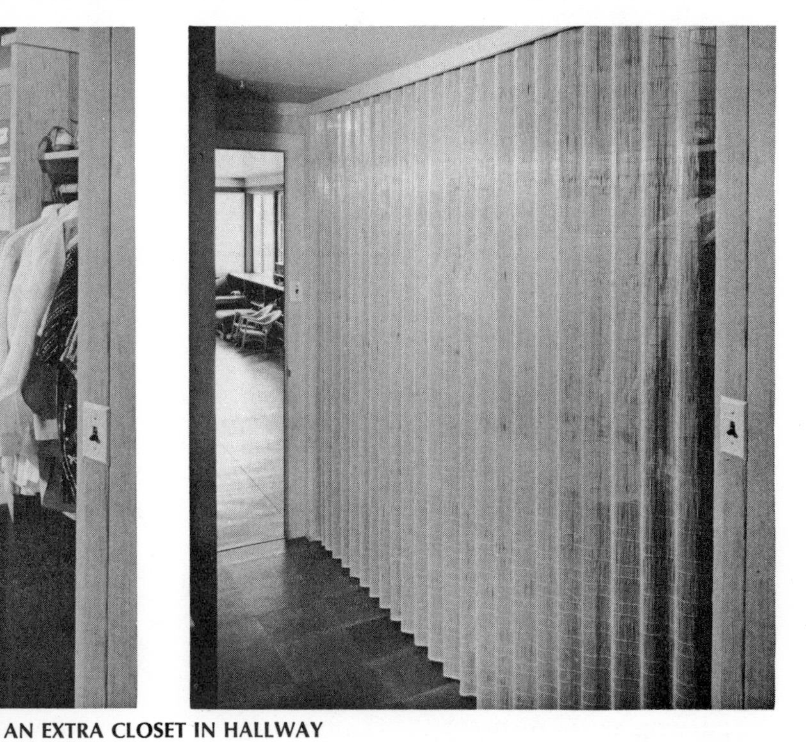

AN EXTRA CLOSET IN HALLWAY

Clothes closet in hall has set of drawers in middle; top of chest serves as a dressing table. Hanging garments are on sides. Note light above chest of drawers. Folding bamboo curtain closes off closet. Archs.: Ives & Hogan.

Dividing closet space so every square foot counts

SHOES ARE OFF THE FLOOR
Closet has high and low bars for sport shirts, jackets. Shoes are easy to see and reach. Design: Floyd Johnson.

COMPACT BEDROOM CLOSET
Shirts hang on high rods, drawers fit underneath. Doors are mirrored on inside. Design: Stuart W. Fletcher.

DRAWERS ARE ABOVE DRESSING TABLE
Drawers above dressing table are for folded items; drawers below hold cosmetics.

17"
14½"
12¾"
Pole
58½"
Concrete slab
12"

EASIER-TO-REACH CLOSET SHELVES
Additional shelf space is gained by lowering clothes bar. Lowered closet floor is covered with vinyl tile. Design: Louis Mazzetto.

SPACIOUS WARDROBE USES TOWEL RACKS

Towel bars are used as tie racks and tie racks are used for hanging belts in this spacious wardrobe. Closet floor slopes up to rear, increasing accessibility and reducing dust problem. Rack holds shoes. Design: Klaus Pfeffer.

GLASS-FRONTED DRAWERS

Folded items are seen at a glance with glass-fronted pull-out drawers.

EGGCRATE PARTITIONS

Socks are placed in egg-crate partitions. Arch.: John Dinwiddie.

NARROW PULL-OUT DRAWERS

Pull-out drawers are built into a narrow section of this wardrobe.

Handbags and shoes...

VERTICAL PARTITIONS FOR HANDBAGS
Cabinet outside walk-in closet has adjustable partitions for changing purse styles. Design: Marge Oppenheimer.

PLASTIC SHOE CONTAINERS
Stacked on top of each other, plastic shoe containers keep shoes accessible. Design: Marge Oppenheimer.

A place for jewelry...

BUILT-IN METAL CASE
Thirty two "small parts" drawers are made of clear plastic; hold collection of jewelry. Design: Lillis and Smith.

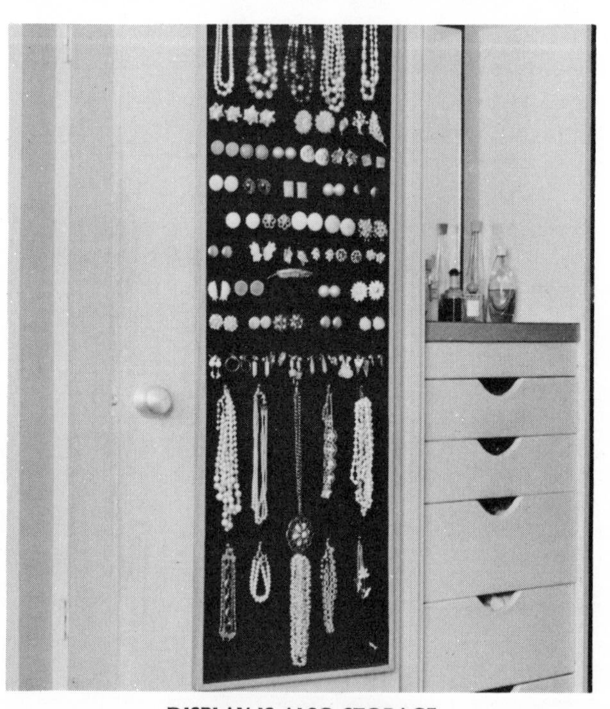

DISPLAY IS ALSO STORAGE
Rack hung on closet door measures 17 to 54 inches. Velvet is attached to face of rack. Design: Lorrin Andrade.

A closet for chore clothes or outdoor garments...

CLOSET FOR WET GEAR
Closet for wet gear is behind door to garage. Heavy ribbed plastic sheet, cut to fit closet floor, catches drips, is easy to clean.

CLOTHES CLOSET IN ENTRYHALL
Boots and garden shoes placed on easy-to-clean flooring. Archs.: Mithum & Associates.

AIR REGISTER HELPS IN DRYING
Warm air register helps dry boots. Shelf top used as seat, for school books. Arch.: William H. Trogdon.

CLOTHES-DRYING CLOSET
Hot air ducts help to dry wet clothing in space next to hot water heater and furnace. Arch.: Jack Sidener.

Storage for

CHILDREN'S CLOTHING, TOYS

Storage walls for varied needs • An easy-to-make wardrobe

Solving shoe storage problems • Built-in beds provide extra storage

Keeping toys off the floor • Storing model railroads • Work areas

When planning storage units for children's rooms, keep in mind that the child will probably be using the same room for years. A baby's room needs only a crib and dresser, whereas a seven-year-old's requirements have greatly multiplied. Flexibility is needed here to accommodate three main types of storage requirements throughout the years of growth and change. These categories are: areas for clothing, recreation or hobby items, and space for educational pursuits. Unless your storage units are keyed to cope with the changes in size and interest, problems will probably occur later.

The general rule for making storage units flexible is to stay away from built-ins. However, built-ins can be your answer if they are equipped with adjustable shelves and adjustable clothes rods. Otherwise, free-standing chests of drawers and closets are easier to modify as your child grows older. The same is true with desk and work or play areas. Simple addition of more work surface and standard storage units saves effort in the long run.

Help the child to help himself

The dream of parents is to have their children handle their own clothes storage. Impossible? Not if you design the storage unit so the child has no trouble opening the door, or reaching hangers and replacing them. Also, drawers that are low enough for replacement of belongings encourage tidiness.

Design the wardrobe closet to allow for the height and reaching distance of your child. For children three to five years of age, place the clothes rod 30 inches off the floor. When the child grows older, raise the rod to 45 inches. Consider the depth of a closet also. It doesn't need to be the full 24 inches required for adults. But if it is this depth from the start, the closet won't need enlarging when the child needs the full space.

Provide for flat or folded clothes with a low chest of drawers or open shelves. The more shallow the drawers, the better. This will prevent heavy loading and the children will have no trouble pulling the drawers open. Also, if every item in the drawer is easy to see, fewer "I can't find it" excuses will be heard.

Solve shoe storage problems in one of two ways. The easiest way is to purchase a metal shoe rack that fits neatly in a closet. Or, you can build a simple rack or partitioned box that fits under hanging clothes.

Another type of shoe rack that will allow for your children's growth resembles a bookcase. It

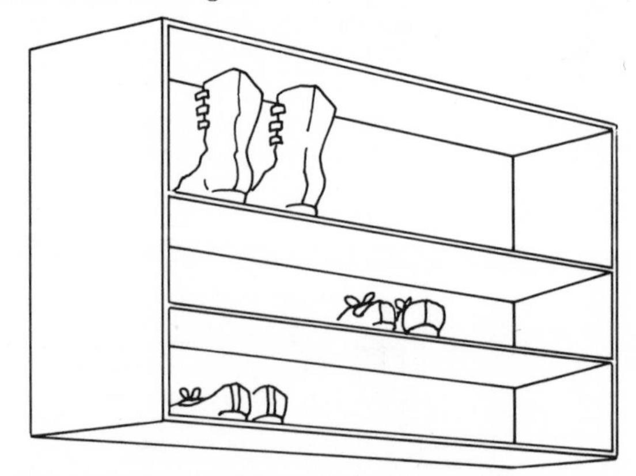

This shoe rack allows for growth

can be made from 1 by 6-inch lumber for the box and shelves and 1/4-inch plywood for the backing. Hang this unit on the wall, a door, or the side of a dresser. The size can be tailored to the number of shoes your children have. Make the shelves high enough for bigger shoes as time passes.

How to keep toys off the floor

The difficulty in storing toys is that they come in a dazzling array of sizes and shapes. Not only do the storage units have to be large enough to handle a variety of toys, but they should be flexible to accommodate the changing interests of your children.

Make the storage boxes simple. A practical way of doing this is to use heavy cardboard boxes. Paint them in bright hues or cover them with boldly designed wallpaper or gift paper. When the boxes become beaten and bedraggled replace them with new containers. You may want something that will last longer and be easy to move around. If so, an easy-to-build, easy-to-use storage box can be made by attaching four plate casters to a 24-inch piece of 3/4-inch plywood. To this board nail four square

Casters make toy box easy to move

wooden boxes. Children can pull the cart around to pick up toys—then slide it into a closet. Toys will also fit in deep bins set under a built-in sofa or window seat.

Whatever method you choose or adapt to your children's needs, be sure to keep the storage unit low to the floor. A child normally plays on the floor, and a unit low enough will make it easier for him to get toys out and replace them. Storage boxes should not be too large, as breakage of toys underneath can result. Also, a convenient-sized box of playthings can be transported easily if you are going on a trip or short visit,

Use open shelves for display toys. Every child has some toys—such as model cars or dolls—that should not be tossed haphazardly into a bin when not in use. And the child usually wants to display them to anyone he can tow into the bedroom. Open shelving is one way of meeting this situation. For best display, you can mount the shelves in a window. If this is not practical—then open shelving along one wall might be the answer. In either case, you may want to keep the shelves low, with the top shelf no higher than your child can reach. But for the mementos or meaningful gifts, you might possibly want to place some shelves higher. Make the shelves sturdy by fastening them to wall studs. In most cases, shelves 12 inches deep will be adequate. But you will probably want to build one or two at least 24 inches deep for the larger toys.

Keep model railroads hidden yet ready for use. Storing model railroads presents a long-term storage problem. It takes time to dismantle a system of tracks, bridges, and tunnels. It also takes time to untangle sections of track that have been stored. Why not keep the train system all set up, yet out of sight when not in use? Just mount the tracks and accessories on a rigid board or table and then devise a means of getting it out of the way when children seek new adventure.

One such device is to have the mounted system swing up into a bookcase with shelves for engines and cars. Another way is to have the set-up mounted on a ping-pong table, so you can reverse the table when you want to use the trains. A third method is to hinge a box-shaped lid to the table. When the box is set down over the train board, it will serve as a work bench. And if none of these suggestions will work—a good arrangement is to

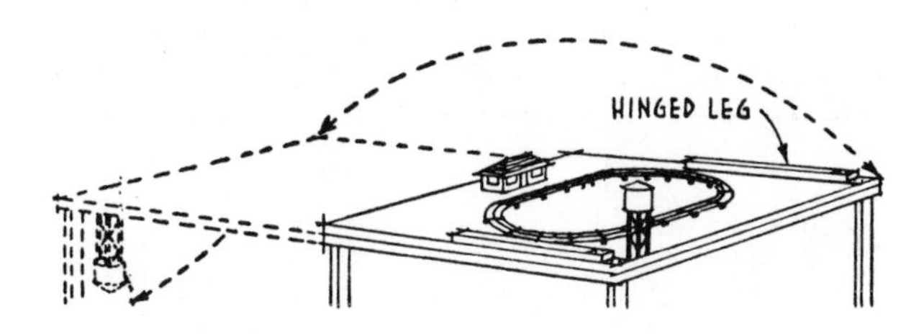

A ping-pong table or a model railroad

make use of the ceiling space in the garage or playroom. The train board can be pulled up to the ceiling by sash cord and pulleys.

Work areas must grow with the child

A desk that grows with the child and is adaptable to changing interests serves as the best work center. Remember that the simple addition of more work surface and storage units will help to minimize this problem.

Commercially-built units or built-ins? The work area is the one exception to the rule of avoiding built-ins for children's rooms. Your child's bedroom may be too small for available commercially-built units, or, the design of the room may be wrong. A built-in working surface might be the only answer. Or, if floor space is at a minimum, consider a wall desk with a fold-out work surface.

Work surfaces must be hardy. Whether commercially-built or designed to fit available space, the working surface must withstand the wear and tear that a child can give. Most hardwoods will wear a long time, but they can be marred, scratched, and gouged. A covering of laminated plastic can be the answer to these considerations.

These storage walls are designed to meet varied needs

STORAGE WALL INCLUDES CLOSET FOR EACH CHILD

Identical built-in units provide ample space for encouraging youngsters to be neat and orderly. Divided storage shelves are in the center section; graduated drawer space below is for clothes and toys. Arch.: Kermit L. Darrow.

COMPLETE WARDROBE UNIT CAN BE CLOSED OFF

Closet has a bank of drawers up to mid-height; upper section for hanging garments. Archs.: Bassetti & Morse.

CLOSET IS IN ROOM DIVIDER

Clothes pole is within easy reach of children; built-in shelves for folded garments. Arch.: George Andrews.

An easy-to-make wardrobe with changeable shelves

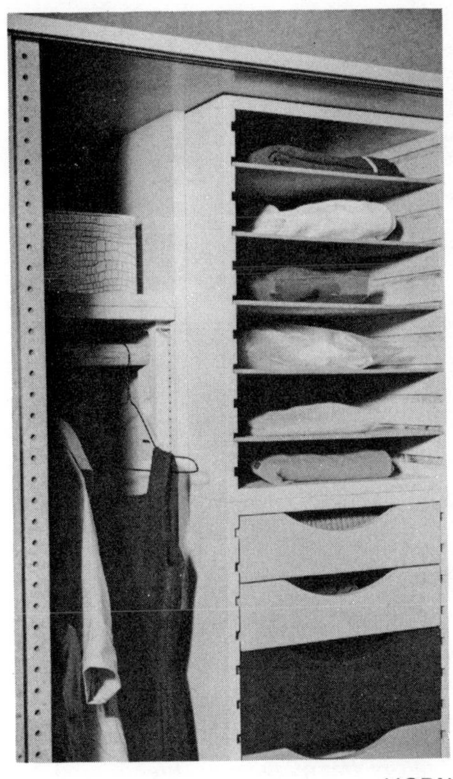

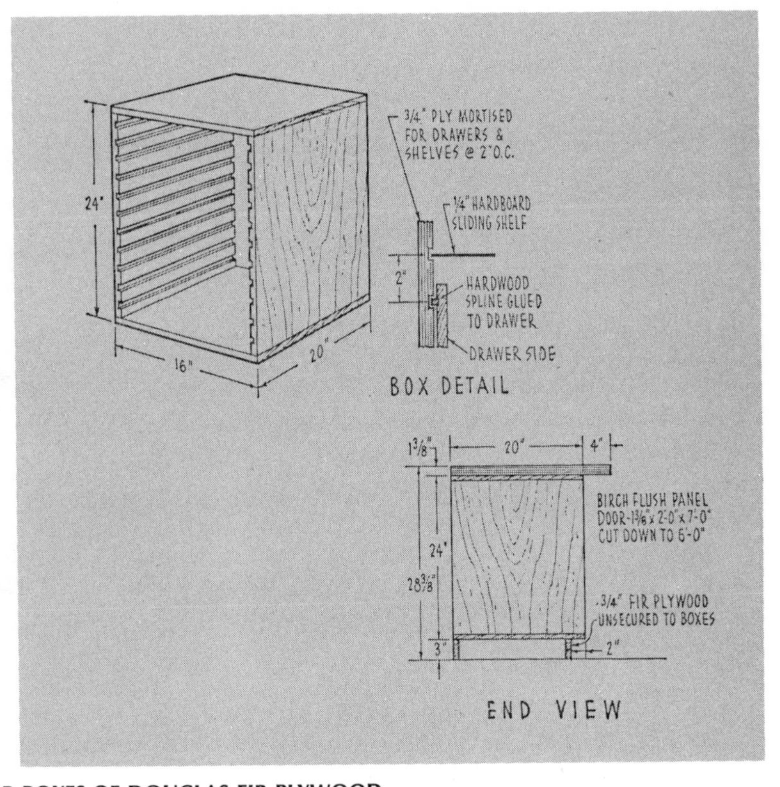

MODULAR BOXES OF DOUGLAS FIR PLYWOOD

Modular boxes stack for wardrobe storage space. Shelves and drawer splines slide in slots every 2 inches. Slots are 1/4-inch deep, 1/2-inch wide. Drawers have 3/4-inch faces, 1/2-inch sides. Bottoms are 1/4-inch hardboard.

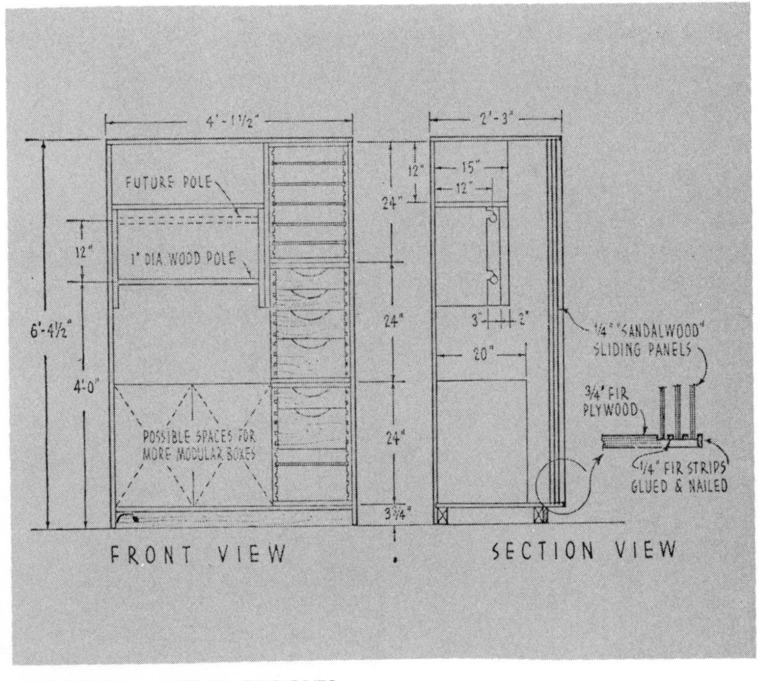

WARDROBE DOORS SLIDE IN GROOVES

Wardrobe doors slide in grooves made by gluing and nailing strips of 1/4-inch vertical grain Douglas fir in rabbeted track area. Height is 76 1/2 inches; width 49 1/2 inches; depth 27 inches. Arch.: Robert Wilmsen.

Built-in beds provide extra storage, free floor for play

TOP BUNK BED IS HIGHER THAN USUAL
Top bunk bed is placed high, allows storage space for bookshelves, bedding. Archs.: Liebhardt and Weston.

PULL-OUT BED FOR GUEST
Pull-out bed for an occasional guest has innerspring mattress, rests on built-in frame. Design: Loren Thompson.

BUILT-IN IS 11-FOOT-LONG BED
Built-in bed holds two 66 by 33-inch youth size mattresses. Lavender spread has box pleats across front and boxed corners. Drawers below are storage space for pillows, blankets, playthings. Design: Loren Thompson.

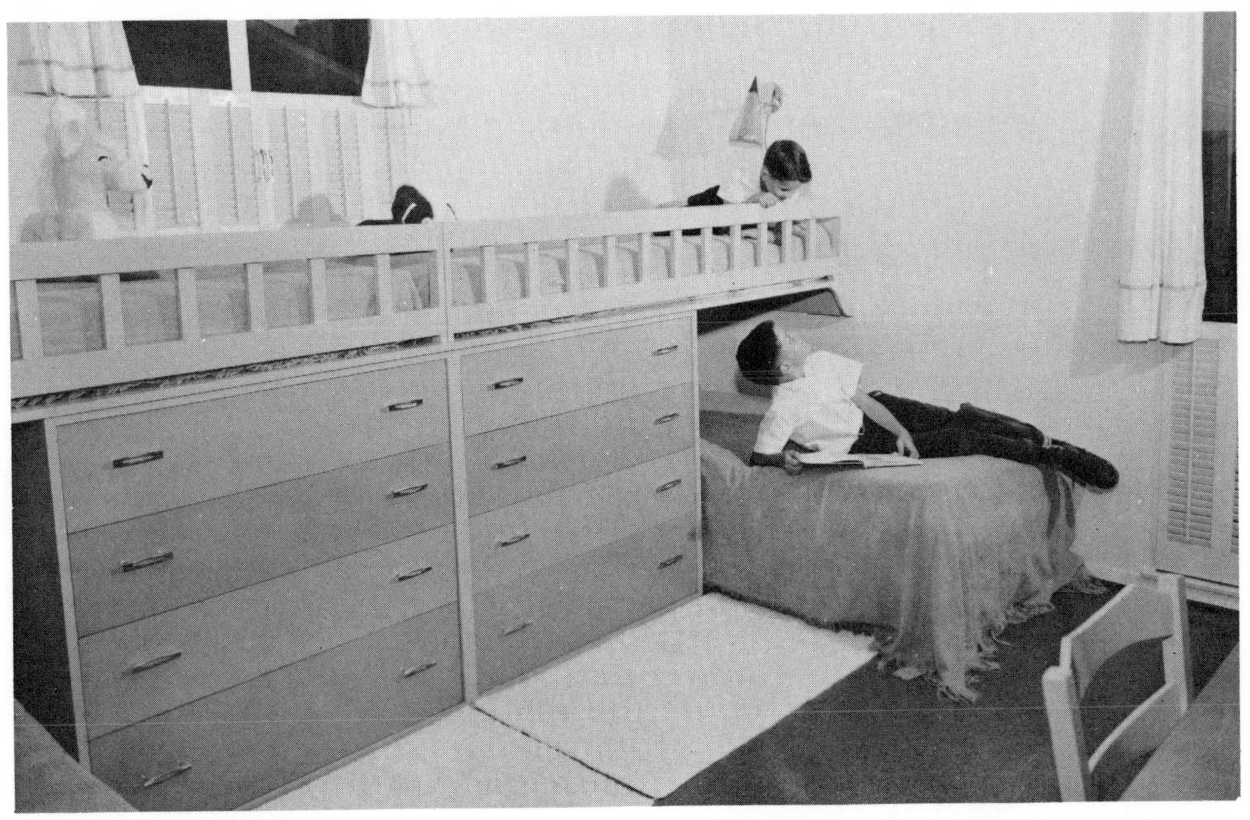

BEDS SLIDE IN AND OUT OF RECESS

Along one wall, twin bunks top a massive $6^1/_2$-foot-wide block of storage drawers. On floor, beds slide in and out of recess on either side. A two-section safety rail runs from wall to wall; can be removed for bed-making.

SPACE UNDER BED USED FOR STORAGE

Roomy storage drawers roll out on rubber-tired wheels under bunk bed; guides, stops keep drawer in position. Design: R. O. Osburn.

UPPER BUNK SUSPENDED FROM BEAM

Top bunk bed rests on ledger strip; foot rests on shelf frame. Design: Dr. Leonard Nevler.

Toys are easy to fetch and easy to put away

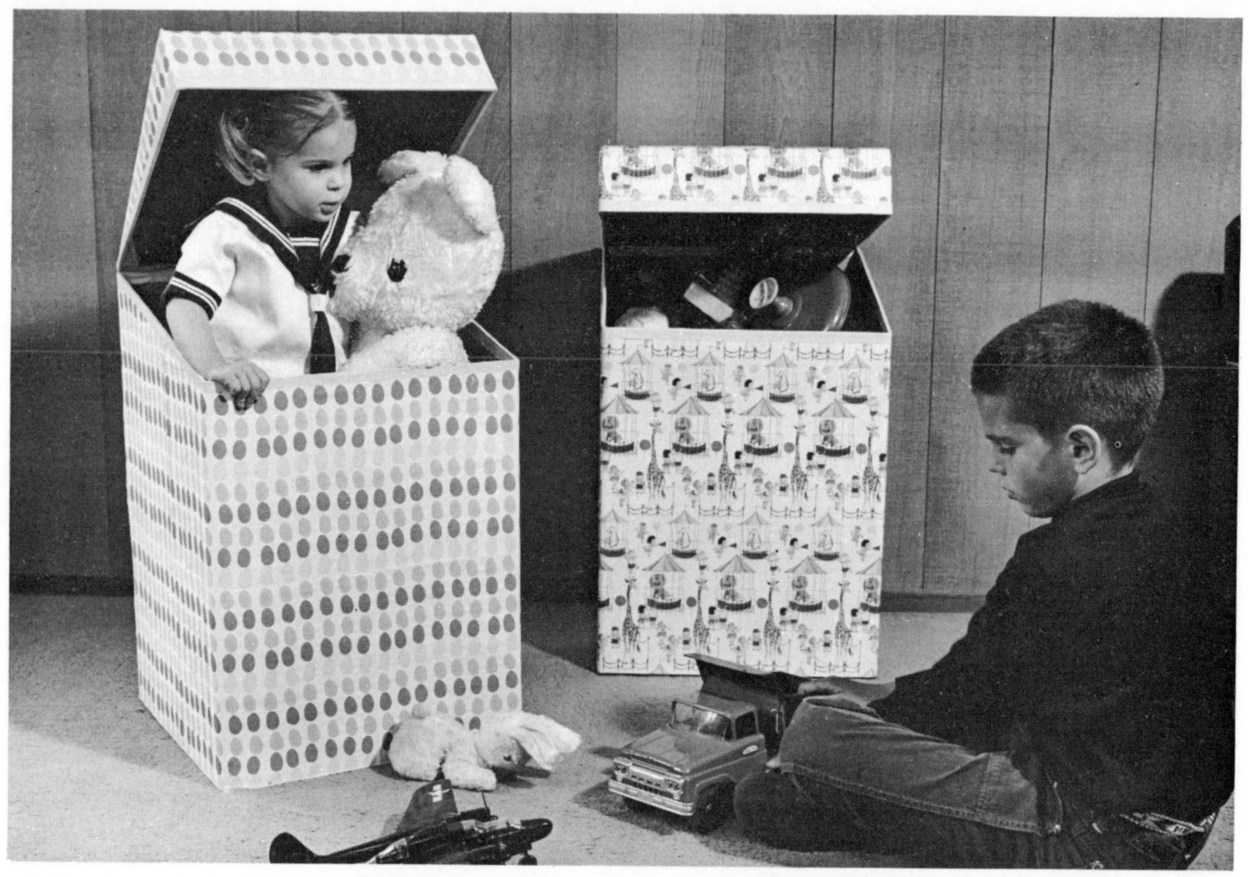

CARDBOARD CARTONS HOLD TOYS OR SMALL PEOPLE

These decorated cardboard cartons hold many toys. The top of sturdy cardboard carton is glued back together; carton is covered with wallpaper; lid is cut about 4 in from top; edges are reinforced with cloth tape.

DISPLAY SHELVES FOR MODELS AND TOYS

Adjustable and interchangeable shelves are made from $^3/_4$-inch plastic-faced plywood; will fit different needs as years pass.

CAN BE PACKED OFF TO COLLEGE

Storage wall can be dismantled, packed off to college later. Arch.: Marshall W. Perrow.

BENCH HAS DRAWERS FOR STORAGE

Bench rolls around on casters, has cushioned seat and pull-out drawers for toys. Design: Dr. Leonard Nevler.

DRAWERS ARE PLASTIC VEGETABLE BINS

Drawers for storage of toys are colored plastic vegetable bins which slide in grooves. Arch.: Robert S. Grant.

COUNTER TOP IS DIVIDED IN SECTIONS

Each section lifts to disclose shallow storage for toys. Bins below provide additional storage, roll on casters.

TOY CHEST ON CASTERS

Toy chest on casters is made of plywood; rolls easily in and out underneath TV set. Arch.: Tucker and Shields.

These train tables pull-up or fold-up—out of the way

RAISED AND LOWERED BY ELECTRIC MOTOR

Train table is lowered by quarter-inch stainless steel cables attached to metal supports that run in channels in center column. In raised position, train table becomes decorative ceiling light panel. Arch.: Douglas W. Rucker.

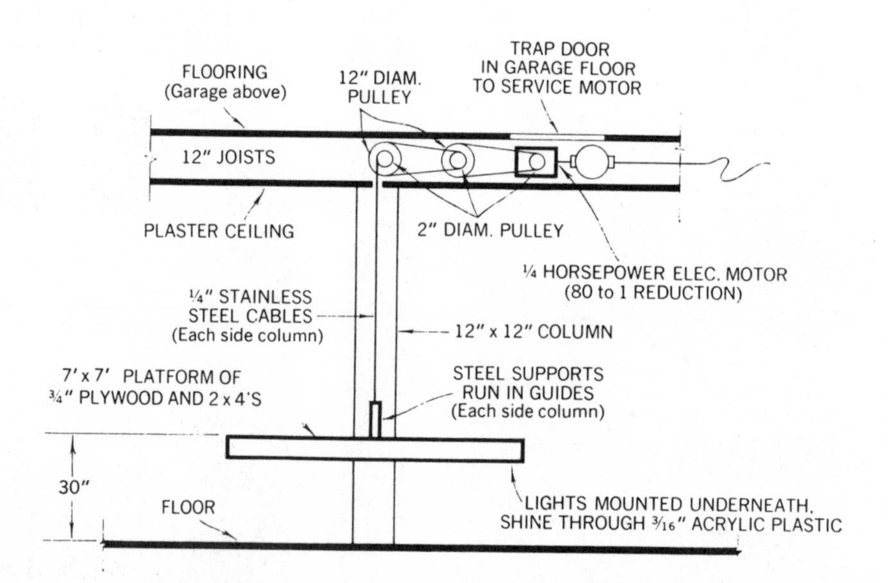

WIRE FROM CEILING SUPPLIES POWER FOR TRAIN

Power for train is supplied through spring-coiled wire from ceiling. The wire stretches out and recoils as the table is raised and lowered. Vertical 2 by 2's bolt over guide channels to take weight off steel cable, for safety.

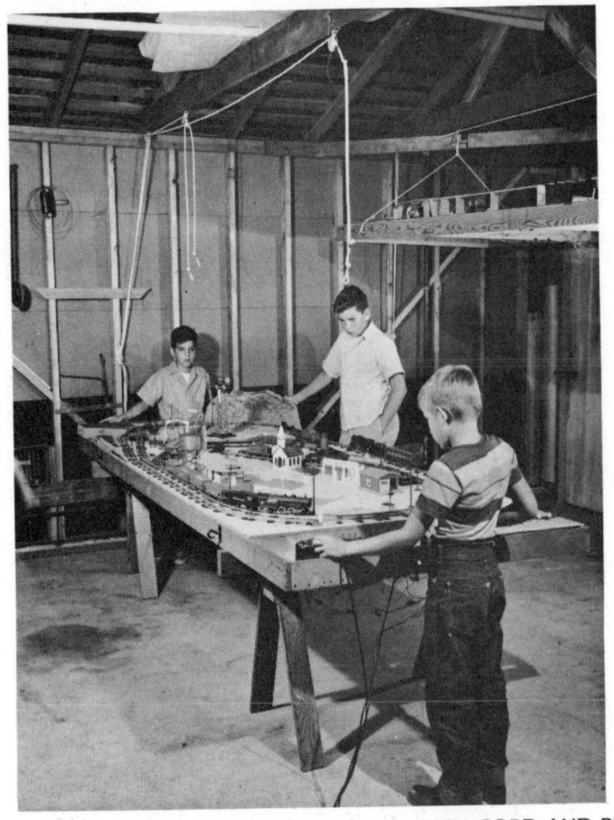

SASH CORD AND PULLEYS DO THE TRICK

Heated garage doubles as play area. Train table is pulled up to the garage ceiling with sash cord and pulleys. Train remains on the tracks and complete layout can be covered with wrapping paper for longer storage periods.

TRAIN TABLE DISAPPEARS AS PART OF WALL

Train board table folds down, supported by two legs at front, shelf ledge at rear. Shelf, extra cars, hang from hooks in perforated hardboard. Folded up, bottom of table is used for picture display. Arch.: R. A. Ettinger.

Here are work areas adaptable to changing interests

THIS DESK GROWS UP WITH THE OWNER

Shown here, table top is 24¾ inches high; later, the entire desk can be turned upside down, so working height is 28¾ inches. Table is made of hollow-core door faced with hardboard; has adjustable shelves.

ROOM IS SHARED BY TWO CHILDREN

Each child has desk space, file-drawer cabinet, desk lamp, adjustable shelf space. Arch.: Kermit L. Darrow.

LIGHT HIDDEN UNDER SHELF

Hidden lumiline tube gives good direct light on desk, indirect on nearby shelves. Shelves can be raised, lowered.

ROOM DIVIDER HAS FOLD-DOWN DESK
Shelves and desk are part of room divider. Partition is centered on window. Desk top is made of plastic-surfaced hardboard.

DESK OCCUPIES SMALL WALL SECTION
Space between entry and closet doors in bedroom is occupied by 3-foot-10-inch desk.

GENEROUS WORK AND STORAGE SPACE
Work area is made from 6-foot-8-inch by 24-inch hollow core door fastened to two drawer chests 30 inches high.

PULL-OUT WORK BOARDS
In small room shared by two boys, a double dresser has pull-out work boards. Design: Mrs. Kent Zimmerman.

Storage for

HI-FI, RECORDS, TELEVISION

Storing records and tapes • Hide-a-ways for the television set

Possible locations for hi-fi • Components housed in a shelf

Music walls • Special requirements for hi-fi equipment

Every family has some sort of entertainment center in the home—whether it be a television set, radio, high fidelity stereo equipment, or tape recorder. Where you install any one of these units depends on the size of the unit and space available in your home. Many people find the easiest solution is to incorporate all entertainment units into one "music wall" built into one wall of the living or family room. Others have extremely limited space and place these units wherever they can.

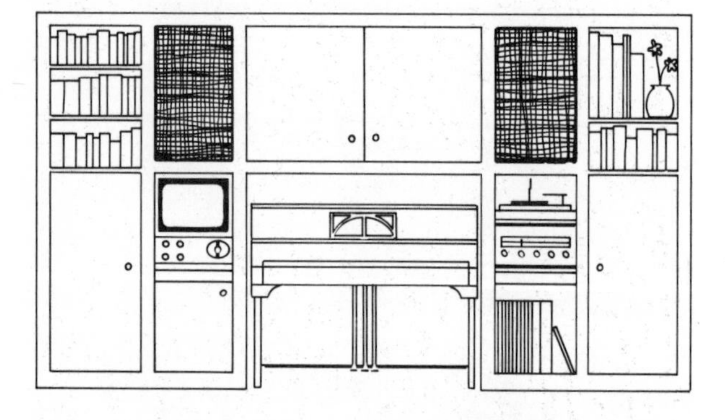

A music wall for varied entertainment

Whatever the situation in your house, here are some ideas for storing hi-fi equipment, records and tapes, and the television set.

Special requirements for hi-fi equipment

Planning storage of a high-fidelity music system involves a unique situation: the components must be stored where they will have proper ventilation and easy accessibility, yet the location must also be excellent from the standpoint of listening enjoyment. Here are some requirements for each piece of equipment that must be considered:

The tuner. First consideration is accessibility for servicing. Another requirement is some ventilation. Relatively little heat build-up can damage this part. A peg board back can provide adequate ventilation. Consider the lead-in when you are deciding where to put the tuner.

The amplifier. Accessibility is a factor here, too, for occasional replacement of tubes. The amplifier generates more heat than any other component and must be well ventilated. Unvented, it can get hot enough to blister the cabinet's finish. A word of caution: Try to avoid putting the amplifier and tuner in the same compartment. Their combined heat could easily damage the tuner and can give a "feedback" noise.

The record changer. A stable, level platform is the record changer's chief requirement. Relatively little vibration can cause a needle to jump the track on a record. Build your shelf solidly. If you put this unit on a pull-out drawer, it must be solidly supported also. The record changer will probably be your largest unit, requiring a shelf about 16 inches square.

The speakers. These units need no ventilation. Whether your speakers are housed in one or more cabinets, the enclosure must be absolutely solid. All joints should be screwed and glued, except for the back. This should be just screwed in place in case of possible removal of the speakers. The material covering the speaker opening should be a loose weave. The proper material can be obtained from sound equipment dealers.

Possible locations for hi-fi

With the above considerations firmly in mind, you can then select the best possible location for your hi-fi installation. Assuming space is limited, here are a few suggestions:

Between the wall studs. This location involves permanent location of some components. Care must be taken to provide adequate space for servicing and ventilation. Doors can be made to conceal the equipment, and also blend in with the rest of the wall paneling.

In free-standing cabinets. If you think of the components as building blocks, you can see the many possibilities in putting them together in a cabinet. Ready-made cabinets can be obtained, either finished or in unassembled form ready to put together and finish. If standard sizes do not fit your needs, construction of a special unit according to your specifications may be the answer.

In a closet. If space is really at a premium you can install all the components on shelves on the back of a solid closet door or on special shelving within the closet.

In a bookcase. All units except the speaker will usually fit in a bookcase that is 12 inches deep and high enough to accommodate the largest unit. Be sure to provide for adequate ventilation.

On a single shelf. Installing stereo on a simple shelf has these advantages: The room's arrangement need not be disturbed; it is easier to build; it can be built to fit your components; you can remove it later if you move or decide to change its location; tuner and amplifier can be stacked together to have a shorter shelf for a small room. Many tuners and amplifiers today have attractive cases and are designed to be out in the open on a shelf. Such placement assures good heat dissipation. Some speakers come complete in their own small wood cabinets; you can set them on the ends of a shelf with none of the problems of mounting four speakers properly in two home-built baffles.

Store records and tapes on edge

A necessary accompaniment to a hi-fidelity sound system is a collection of records and tapes to be stored as near the record player and tape recorder as possible.

A cabinet shelf 13 inches high and as deep will enable you to stand all records on edge. A shelf 8 inches high will be adequate for storing all tapes. Simple hardboard dividers placed every few inches will make it easy to find records. A closet partitioned with shelves could provide you with a similar area. Even a bookshelf can suffice for storing records, provided the shelf depth is adequate. You may have to move some books elsewhere to make room for the records—but then, books can go almost anywhere and records cannot.

Pull-out bins are the answer for storing records and tapes label-side out. These bins can be placed on pull-out shelves or simply be placed on a shelf for

Record labels are easy to see

easy removal. Made of plywood or just a simple cardboard box, these containers have the advantage of being placed in available space.

Commercial cabinets or stands are available in various sizes and shapes. Some cabinets are made of wood-veneer and have removable wire separators to hold the records on edge. There are roll-about stands with 12 or more record sections and other shelves for accessories. And if you are completely cramped for space, a simple innovation for storing records is the record pole. Reaching from floor to ceiling, this pole has three racks that will adjust for height. The pole can be faced in different directions.

Ideas for concealing the television set

If you feel that a television screen, like a movie screen, should be hidden when there's no show on, you may be interested in these ideas for concealing the television set.

You can build a cabinet to house your TV set. This need not be a large, permanently located fixture—a small roll-around cabinet for a portable TV may be just suited for your needs. The top of the cabinet can also serve as an extra table top or serving tray. You can cut out a portion of wall between two rooms and insert a portable TV set that can swivel around to face either room; you may wish to have a small door on each side that can close off the set when it is being viewed in the other room.

Ventilation is a must. Before you embark on any project of your own, consult a competent television technician to get his recommendations for proper set ventilation. Ideally, the enclosure should be vented at the bottom, back, and top. In snug situations you may have to install a small fan that operates when the set is on.

These music centers are built into the walls

ALL MUSIC COMPONENTS ARE BEHIND CABINET DOORS

Ten-foot-wide music wall provides ample separation for stereo speakers (upper left and right). Record cabinets have hardboard separators. Amplifiers housed in open cabinet (center); turntable in drawer. Arch.: C. M. Butler.

WALL HOUSES TELEVISION, PIANO, RECORD PLAYER

Cabinets in ceiling-height storage wall now house television, piano, record player. Later it can accommodate stereo equipment, books, games. Light comes from fixtures overhead. Archs.: Thomas & Baar.

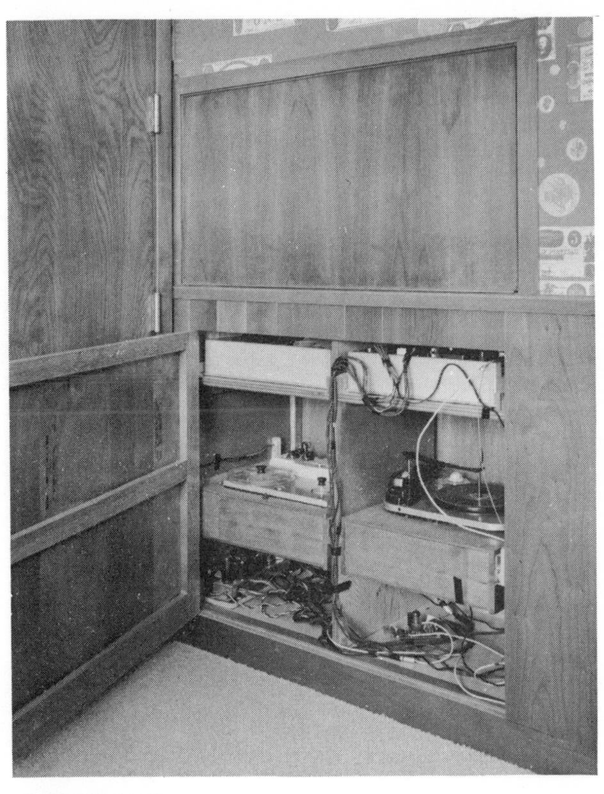

DESIGNED TO SERVE TWO ROOMS

Music center is built into a wall between a living room and den. Speakers face the living room, to hear music in den, a panel is dropped between the rooms. Components easy to reach for repair. Design: S. C. Robinson.

LOW MUSIC WALL

Low music wall contains tape recorder, turntable, radio, tuner, speakers, record storage. Arch.: Walter L. Reichardt.

TURNTABLE IN SWING-OUT CABINET

Bookcase wall holds hi-fi; speaker; record changer in swing-out cabinet.

These components are housed in a shelf

SPEAKERS ARE AT EITHER END OF SHELF

Single shelf houses high fidelity stereophonic equipment. It holds a compact speaker cabinet at each end, record changer, tuner and amplifier. Center of shelf has two cork-covered doors to protect changer from dust.

Tape and record player cabinet serve as room divider

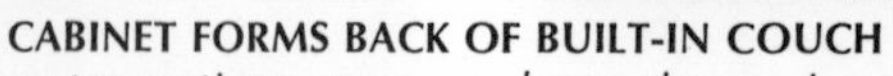

CABINET FORMS BACK OF BUILT-IN COUCH

Low cabinet has five sections. Three center sections open at top for tape and record-player controls; two on ends have doors, house records, tapes. Cabinet is framework for seating arrangement. Arch.: Paul Sterling Hoag.

Records and player hide out in a closet

SHELVES AND BINS FOR RECORD STORAGE

Shelves and bins provide record storage in unused closet. Upper shelves with dividers hold albums; bins on rollers hold single records. Doors for upper and lower sections open separately. Archs.: Holmes & Sellery.

Hi-fi speakers are concealed in an entryway closet

SPEAKERS ARE MOUNTED ON PLYWOOD

Decorative vertical panel at the foot of the stairs is speaker cloth behind Philippine mahogany grid, which conceals hi-fi speakers. Speakers, mounted on plywood behind grid, are located in closet. Arch.: Alfred Preis.

How to build in (or even hide) your TV...

TELEVISION SET BUILT INTO WALL
Special entertainment wall contains this unit. Heat from set escapes through holes in cabinet above nearby vent.

SET SHARES DIVIDER CABINET
Flush panel pulls across front of set in divider cabinet shared with record player. Archs.: Liebhardt & Weston.

COUNTER HOUSES TV, STORAGE CABINETS
New room contains counter housing storage cabinets, TV. Arch.: Raymond Lloyd.

ROLL-AROUND CABINET FOR PORTABLE TV
Roll-around cabinet for portable television set has fold-up doors and plastic top for doubling as small serving buffet.

TELEVISION ROTATES ON CASTERS

Casters on piece of hardboard rotate television. Protruding pin under set rides in slot so TV doesn't roll off into the room. Design: Roy Woenne.

PANEL SWINGS BACK

Panel is covered with painting, swings open on piano hinge to reveal set.

BEHIND LOUVERED DOORS

Sliding shelf brings TV out for better viewing. Design: W. H. Doelling.

ABOVE DESK IN STORAGE CABINETS

Master bedroom has built-in desk, work counter, and storage cabinets. Middle doors above the desk open to reveal the television. Arch.: Stanley G. Gould.

Storage for

HOUSEHOLD OFFICE SUPPLIES

Practical locations • Storing the typewriter • Planning drawer space around a desk

Importance of book shelves • Specialized storage facilities

An office area in the home should be planned so that it will accommodate such items as a typewriter, books, a filing cabinet, and an assortment of pencils, pens, paper, and other writing supplies. A desk or similar work area is the fulcrum around which the storage is arranged. Undoubtedly, the ideal arrangement is to have a room set aside as an office that would work on the same general principle as the old-fashioned roll-top desk (by closing the door you could have all the clutter magically disappear). But few families can make an entire room expendable for this purpose. Therefore, what's the next best step? Many homeowners simply set aside one or more small areas where the "family accountant" can write checks, store tax records, etc. Where space is really at a premium, a table top that folds back against the wall may be the answer.

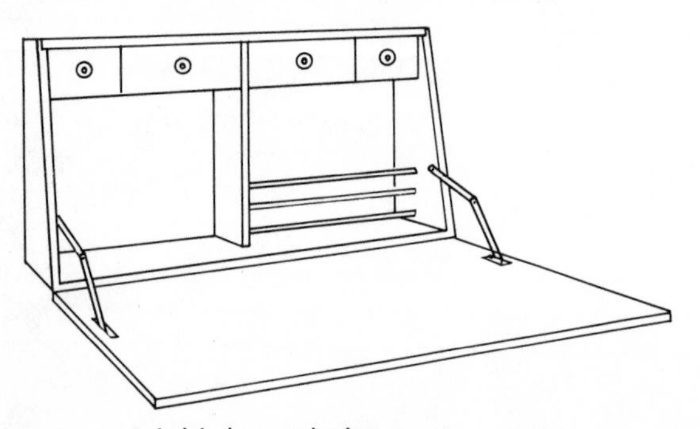

A fold-down desk top saves space

Choose a practical location

Prime considerations for locating the home office are:

. . . location in relation to the rest of the house
. . . amount of storage space required or needed
. . . convenience for the one who uses it most

The living room often has enough free wall space to be given over to a desk or work area. In many homes (particularly those that also have a family room) the living room is a sanctuary from most of the family's hour-to-hour activities. However, providing a unit that blends in with the rest of the furnishings and decor in this area can be a problem. And keeping the working surface in order may be a frustrating experience, especially if you are suddenly interrupted by unexpected guests.

The den or family room can be a practical location for some families. It depends upon several factors, two of the most important being: 1) number of children in the household and their ages and activities; 2) location of the television set. Television viewing and home office work are seldom a happy blend. However, if the family room is big enough, the desk unit might be placed at one end and the television set at the other. Depending on how adept you are at concentrating with a certain amount of background noise, this arrangement might be satisfactory.

The bedroom is one location that usually can be closed off to provide a quiet place to work. However, it can also be an area that is already cramped for space. Here, as in the case of children's rooms, a built-in working surface might be the only answer. Or, a wall desk that can be folded down for use may provide enough working area.

The dining room or dining area is often a very convenient place to do paperwork at home. Dining tables offer one obvious advantage: a generous-sized working surface. Also, the dining area is completely traffic-free most of the time. A disadvantage is that you may have to store the typewriter and other paraphernalia in another part of the house—unless there is a dining room cabinet or buffet with a spare drawer or two.

The kitchen is often overlooked for home office use, but it may contain a breakfast bar, a small table, or a little nook or cranny around the telephone where paperwork can be done efficiently. A nearby drawer or shelf can be used to store the paraphernalia that goes with home office work.

Store supplies within easy reach

Your individual needs determine the size of the work area. Once you have found adequate working space, plan your storage around this working center so everything is within easy reach.

A typewriter can be stored on top of the work surface (remember that this cuts down on working space), on a free-standing cart that can be wheeled out of the way, or on a pull-out or pop-up stand that folds into the desk. Whatever method is right for you, remember that a standard model typewriter requires a space 20 inches deep, 22 inches wide, and 12 inches high. A portable requires a space 16 inches deep, 16 inches wide, and 10 inches high.

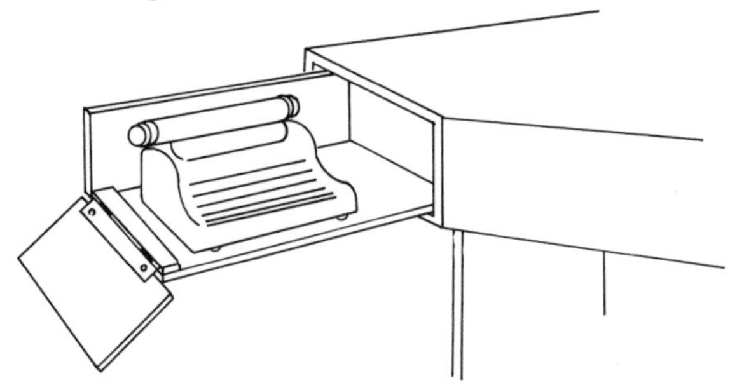

Pull-out shelf holds typewriter

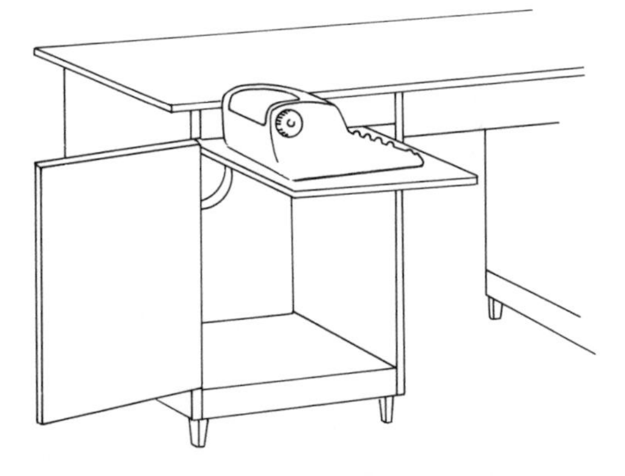

Typewriter pops up—folds back into desk

Filing cabinets can be useful for storing documents and important papers. Cabinets of all sizes—for $8^1/_2$ x 11-inch papers on down to 3 x 5-inch cards—can be purchased for keeping everything at your fingertips. The larger files require a space 26 to 30 inches deep. Be sure to plan for enough space around the cabinet for pulling out the drawers and having room to move around easily.

Drawer space around a desk can be valuable for storing carbon paper, ink pads, pencils, paper clips, and other small items. Chests of drawers can be purchased to fit a basic desk frame. Or, wood or plastic units may provide adequate storage space. Most commercially-made units come equipped with these facilities.

Book shelving is important for a home office. Binders, reference books, bulletins, catalogs, and the telephone book can be stored near at hand. For this part of storage around the working surface, you can make the bookshelves as part of the desk or hang them independently on a facing wall. Either way, consider the possibility of converting a section of shelving to pigeon holes for holding miscellaneous items.

If home is your place of business...

The artist, craftsman, photographer, or salesman who uses his home as his office usually requires specialized storage facilities. Naturally, the facilities differ widely in their design and amount of space required because of the difference in tools of the trade.

A work bench or table need not be built-in. Why not consider the use of a solid-or-hollow-core door (builders supply store), a metal mess table (sporting goods store), or even a ping-pong table (sporting goods store). For sit-down height (29 to 31 inches), these adaptations can be mounted on storage chests, kitchen base cabinets, or filing cabinets. For stand-up or high stool-height tables (36 to 40 inches), the table can be mounted on high sawhorses and large storage units.

Working and reference materials should be handy to the work table. For large sheets of paper, vertical dividers work well. Using wood or plywood strips at each end (or top and bottom) which are grooved at 1-inch intervals, the dividers can be removed to enlarge each compartment. A map cabinet is also a good device for storing flat sheets—and useful, too, for storing quantities of almost any kind of small tools and other items. A smaller version of the map cabinet is a machinist's tool chest; its many drawers in several depths can hold a whole arsenal of small materials.

8 possible locations for your household office

BUILT-IN UNIT IN LIVING ROOM
Fireplace wall has built-in desk, storage drawers, shelves for books. Desk top folds up to conceal clutter. Arch.: Walter Widmeyer.

IN CORNER OF FAMILY ROOM
Home office has built-in desk, shelf space, double doors. Archs.: Bystrom and Greco.

TUCKED INTO HALL ALCOVE
Desk is built around file drawers; storage above on shelves. Arch.: Helen Rysdale.

WHEN MASTER BEDROOM HAS SPACE
An adjacent dressing room gives master bedroom extra wall space for built-in home office, storage cabinets. Archs.: Benton & Park.

OFF CORNER OF DEN
Closet-sized office opens off a corner of the den, contains desk, file and drawers. Design: John F. Jennings.

IN A CORNER OF THE KITCHEN
Old letter holder above desk has series of pigeonholes for filing miscellany; also forms shelf for cookbooks.

GUEST ROOM AND OFFICE IN ONE
Supported by angle braces, laminated plastic counter in guest room provides work space. Design: Cliff May.

A CONVERTED UTILITY AREA
Converted utility room has counter 36 inches high so appliances can be installed later. Design: John Garmany.

Supplies are easy to reach

PARTITIONED DRAWERS FOR SUPPLIES, RECORDS
Drawers below desk are partitioned for stationery, supplies, cancelled checks. Design: Marge Oppenheimer.

FILE CABINET FITS INTO CLOSET
Standard file cabinet near kitchen office backs into a storage closet; front sits flush with kitchen wall.

BOOKSHELVES ARE ABOVE DESK
Desk-bookcase unit has fold-down desk. Beneath the desk are pull-out file drawers, storage for typewriter.

TYPEWRITER POPS UP
Typewriter is stored below desk; pops up when needed. Storage cabinets, drawers are within easy reach.

Place of business is home

VERTICAL DIVIDERS HOLD CANVASES
In artist's studio, slots in wall store canvases. Note slots divided in half. Design: Dennis, Slavsky & Whitaker.

STORAGE CLOSET FITTED TO MATERIALS
Studio for mosaicist has storage closet designed to accommodate needed materials. Archs.: Terry and Moore.

MAP CABINETS SUPPORT WORKING TABLE
Two tiers of map cabinets for supplies support 13-foot table in this working studio. Arch.: William Hempel.

STORAGE IS HANDY TO DRAWING BOARD
Studio has storage for supplies, reference materials handy to drawing board. Design: John Matthias.

Storage for

FIREWOOD

Fireside lockers • Storing firewood on different floor levels

Toting boxes for firewood • Size of storage cabinet

Spraying storage box for destructive pests

A fireplace needs fuel—lots of it. The homeowner also has a need—where to store this fuel. A portable woodbox may be all you need, if the fireplace is not used very often. But if you relish long, enjoyable fires that last through the evening, built-in wood storage will eliminate unwelcome trips to the woodpile.

Ways to be practical

There are many practical ways to provide for wood storage. Of course, some of the ideas presented below can be more costly than others.

A fireside locker with a door that opens outside or into the garage can be a convenient arrangement. The wood can be stacked neatly in place without making several trips in and out of the house. If this arrangement fills your needs, it must also fill the Uniform Building Code requirements. The Code requires that a woodbox opening into a garage or carport have a solid core door with a self-closing apparatus—even if the carport is open on three sides.

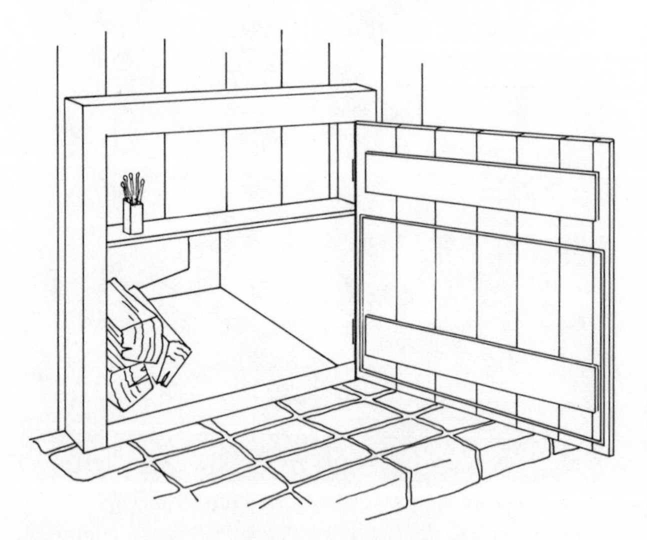

Fireside locker saves trip to garage

A cantilevered hearth or a recessed hearth often provides the easiest solution to storing firewood. Orderly stacking will eliminate the need for an enclosure. However, if you want the wood to be covered, a simple fire screen will do the job and also give the impression of a double fireplace.

A cabinet in a wall near the fireplace is another method. You can balance the cabinet door with other room cabinets or conceal it in wood paneling. Take a look around your fireplace area for possible hideaways. Perhaps the bottom part of a bookcase could be utilized. Or, an inconspicuous door below a window could open to an outside storage box.

Storing wood in the basement, yet having it easily accessible near the fireplace, is a unique arrangement. This involves a winch and an elevator. Logs can be tossed into the basement through a trap door. Here they can be split and stacked. A dumbwaiter—just an open-sided box on cables—can be worked by hand winch to lift the logs to the living-room level. All you need at this level is an opening to the dumbwaiter, which acts as the storage box.

Mind the beetles

Simple storage of firewood is not the final solution. Other features and precautions must be considered. The storage box must work for you by encouraging the building of fires and their upkeep. It must also keep destructive pests (brought in with the firewood) in a quarantined state. The following suggests how to handle both situations.

Make the cabinet wide or deep enough to hold the largest logs you plan to use. And make it big enough to hold enough firewood for several hours or several days. As an added convenience, you might want to build a small shelf in the woodbox to hold matches, paper, or gloves. A simple plywood shelf is easy to install, but you may prefer one made of wire screening. Dividing the cabinet into two sections also helps to keep the kindling separated from the logs.

Prevent beetles from making their homes in your firewood. This is a major consideration. The Cerambycid Beetle commonly attacks oak firewood that has been freshly cut. What if this pest left the firewood in favor of your favorite shade tree or the small sapling that is just starting its climb to the sky? To eliminate this possibility, here are two precautions:

Spraying the storage box with any household insecticide is probably the simplest solution.

Lining the storage box with sheet metal will give you a longer lasting protection. However, this lining must be installed carefully so that there isn't the smallest opening. Beetles can make the tiniest hole bigger very quickly.

These fireside lockers store firewood close at hand

CABINET FOR FIREWOOD OPENS TO OUTSIDE WOODBOX

Wood supply is convenient to fireplace; can be filled without repeated trips into room. Interior has shelf for newspapers, matches. Note metal weatherstripping on opening to outside. Design: George R. Bartholick.

BUILT-IN FIRESIDE WOODBOX

Woodbox is filled with box on a hoist that can be lowered into basement for loading. Design: Norris Gaddis.

WOOD STORAGE BUILT INTO MASONRY

Wood storage is built into the masonry for appearance; has door in back for loading. Design: W. S. Hayden.

Visually a double firepit, but one side stores the wood

FUEL BIN ACCESSIBLE FROM OUTSIDE
Fuel compartment on left is accessible from outside. Fire-screen slides on track. Design: Sewall Smith.

STORAGE BIN ON RIGHT HALF OF FIREPLACE
Wood storage bin shares half of long, raised fireplace unit brass fire curtain. Design: Young and Richardson.

This storage box holds two firewood toting boxes

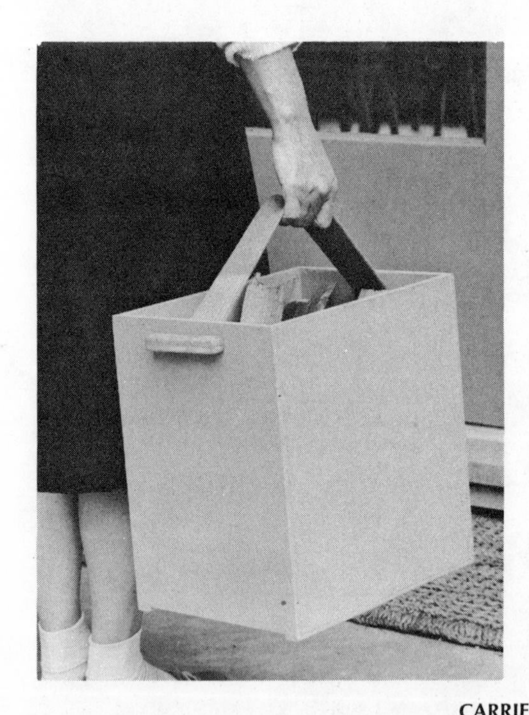

CARRIED BY COTTON WEBBING STRAP
En route, cotton webbing strap is convenient handle. Kindling and logs are pre-cut to 13-inch box height. At fireside, box drawer (partly pulled out) holds firewood; smaller one (to left) holds kindling. Design: Roy Halsey.

Here are ways to store firewood on different floor levels

PASS-THROUGH FROM GARAGE FLOOR IN HILLSIDE HOUSE

Garage of hillside home is higher than house. It adjoins living room, so pass-through was easy to install. Logs stack on garage floor. Pass-through door is covered with same grass cloth as wall. Design: Harold Sylvester.

1 *Logs tossed into basement through trap door. They are split, stacked under the steps.*

2 *Dumbwaiter is open-sided box on cables. Worked by hand winch, it lifts kindling and logs.*

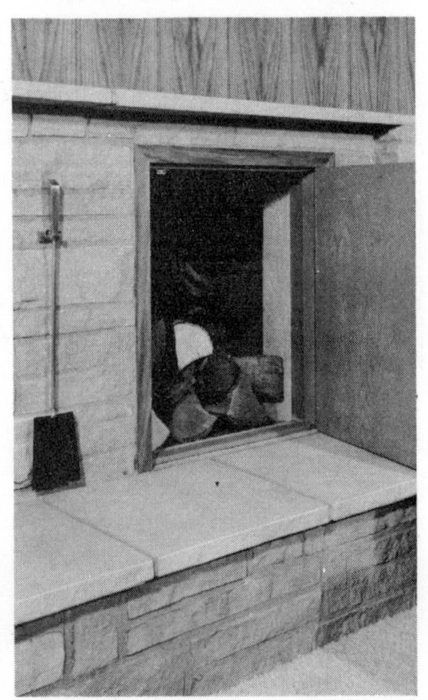

3 *Dumbwaiter wood box when raised to living room near fireplace. Design: S. C. Robinson.*

Storage for

BOTTLED WINES

Ways to store wines, simply or elegantly • The wine cabinet

Storage in a chest of drawers • An easy-to-build wine rack

Converting a closet into a wine cellar

A good home wine cellar requires nothing more than a place for storing your own private supply of wines. You don't need much space. Any shelf, closet, or corner can be made into a wine cellar. But no matter what your choice, there are a few strict requirements. One is that the wine should be kept in a place away from direct sunlight. There should be no vibration or movement. The temperature should remain fairly even—ideally, between 50° and 60°. And the bottles should be placed horizontally on their sides or tilted down slightly (this is to keep the corks moist and airtight). For the connoisseur of wines who desires more specific information for keeping his valuable wines, check with The Wine Institute, 717 Market St., San Francisco, California.

Which arrangement fits your needs?

With the above considerations firmly implanted in your mind, you should be able to adapt one of the following suggestions to fit your individual needs.

A time-honored wine rack is an ideal arrangement for storing wines, wherever space is not at a premium. And it can also be adapted to fit in unusual spots—such as underneath a stairway. Plywood is all you need to make this storage unit.

The rack consists of two vertical 1" x 8" side pieces and a horizontal 1" x 8" top with several rack boards on both front and back as shown. The scalloped rack boards can be notched into the two side pieces or simply nailed or screwed to their edges. The height and length of the rack can be made to suit your desires. The scallops for the back racks should be $3\frac{1}{2}$ inches wide and $1\frac{1}{2}$ inches deep to fit the base of bottles. Scallops for the front racks should be $1\frac{1}{2}$ inches wide and 1 inch deep to fit the necks of bottles. Note that the front scallops start $3\frac{1}{2}$ inches from the end of the crosspiece and continue at $3\frac{1}{2}$ inch intervals, while back scallops start $2\frac{1}{2}$ inches from the end and continue at $1\frac{1}{2}$ inch intervals.

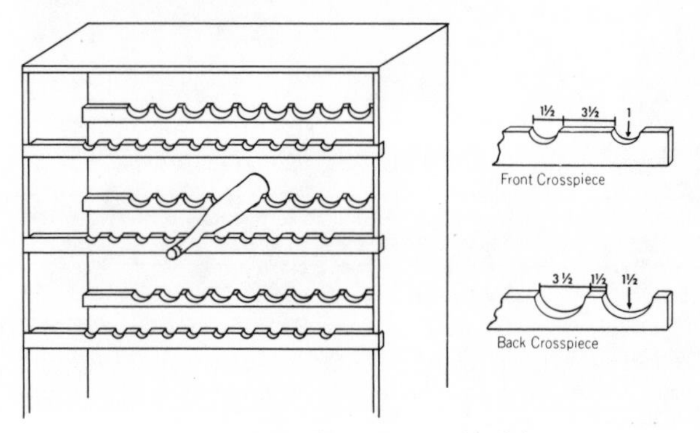

Wine rack is easy to build

The completed rack can be free-standing or fastened to the wall. In either case, it should be set away from a wall—a distance of approximately 3 inches. This will allow the base of the bottles to extend slightly over the back rack.

A chest of drawers is often an easy solution to the challenge of finding space for storing wine. Even if you are not searching for space, this plan makes an excellent place for keeping most frequently served wines easily at hand. After finding the chest

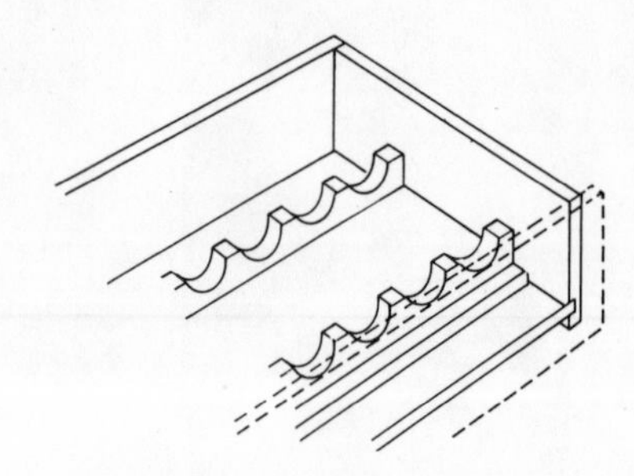

A chest of drawers keeps wines handy

of drawers, all you have to do is to provide the racks. This is easily accomplished by measuring the width of the drawers, cutting a 1" x 8" piece of lumber accordingly for the base and also cutting a 1/2" x 2" piece of molding for the racks. Of course, the molding must be scalloped for holding the bottles firmly in place. Make sure that the base of the rack fits snugly against the side of the drawers and will not move about.

A spare closet is an ideal storage unit for wines in an apartment or small home. Converting a closet into a wine cellar is relatively easy. Just make sure that the closet is at least 14 inches deep. If the closet has shelves, just add the scalloped cross-pieces. If it doesn't, then 1 x 6 boards for your side pieces and 1/2" x 2" scalloped molding will work for almost any size closet. Once again, the racks should be placed so that there is at least 3 inches space between the rack and the wall.

The wine cabinet is another relatively simple solution to wine storage. With this arrangement, you can make use of the space within a cabinet, chest, or bookcase. No nailing is required. As shown in the drawing, the beveled edges of diagonally placed boards provide the support. Space between any existing shelves should be at least 14" deep. The width is not as important because 1" x 12" boards can divide the space into sections.

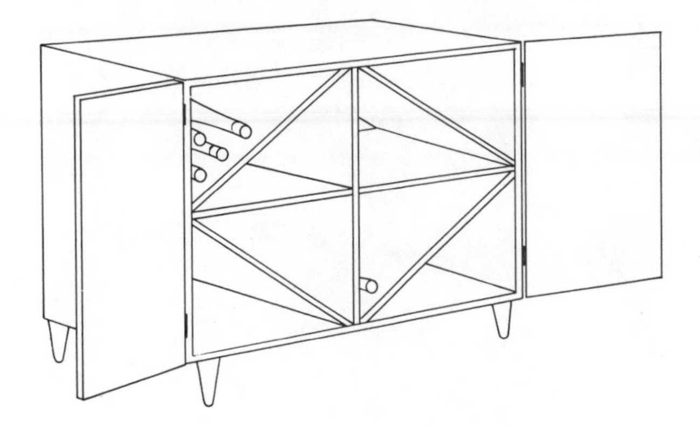

No nailing is required for wine cabinet

This wine cellar is a cool cavern dug out of a hillside

BENEATH A STEEL-REINFORCED CONCRETE PATIO SLAB

This large walk-in cellar dug out of a hillside provides the ideal solution for storing a collection of vintage wines at perfect temperatures. Wine rack against left wall is made of 4-inch clay drain tiles set in concrete.

Here are ways to store wines, simply or elegantly...

THE CASE THE WINE CAME IN
The cardboard case wine comes in can be placed on a cool garage floor in shade, with bottles horizontal.

RACKS ADJUST TO FIT DIFFERENT CABINETS
Accordion-type wine rack can adjust to fit inside many different cabinets. Liqueurs are stored on shelf above.

WINE RACK MADE OF KOA WOOD
Reaching to the ceiling on the cool side of a lanai, this handsome and sturdy wine rack is made of koa wood, screwed to wall.

TRANSFORMED INTO WINE CELLAR
Spanish cabinet is transformed into wine cellar by adding simple wood diagonals.

STORED IN DIVIDED CABINET
Cabinet in storage counter next to dishwasher and bar sink houses divided unit for wines; can fit anywhere.

IN A DEEP STORAGE WALL
Narrow wall space in kitchen is utilized for built-in wine rack. Corner is cool and shady. Design: Fred Blair Green.

WINE STORAGE USING CONCRETE BLOCKS
Short lengths of mailing tubes are placed on plywood shelves supported by concrete blocks which work well as storage dividers.

STORED IN DRAIN TILES
Bottles fit into drain tiles, are stored in basement. Archs.: Beal, Bidwell & Macky.

Storage for

HOME WORKSHOPS

Hanging hand tools • Storing large power tools

Keeping lumber off the floor • A workbench for a boy craftsman

Organizing general miscellany

Location of a workshop—particularly of the woodworking variety—can be a headache. Even if a small bench will suffice as far as actual working surface is concerned, the question of where and how to store tools, lumber, and other materials will take some special planning. In many homes, the garage usually ends up being the most likely spot for locating the workshop. Considering that this location has to be shared with the family car, camping equipment, and other bulky items, there may not be much space left over for a workshop. Many home craftsmen are able to add to the house or build a separate building so they can have their own private domain. However big or small, here are some suggestions for organizing your workshop area.

Keep tools tidy—prevent damage

Unorganized tool storage inevitably damages tools. This doesn't need to happen. All you have to do is space your tools far enough apart to forego fumbling after the wanted item. Since most toolboxes do not lend themselves to this type of organization, here are suggestions for storing tools in other ways:

Hand tools should be hung. To serve you best, most hand tools should be hung in neat order on the wall above the work bench. With this arrangement, it is not difficult to grab whatever tools are needed without interrupting the flow of work.

There are two schools of thought about storing tools on a wall. One favors open shelves or hooks. The other puts the tools behind doors where they stay cleaner and are locked away. The best solution is often a compromise of having most-used tools in view and all others enclosed. In the open or enclosed, here are some ideas that can be adapted to fit your needs.

A perforated hardboard or plywood panel mounted above the workbench is often the easiest solution. The placement of tools on the wall panel should be determined by the frequency of use. For perforated hardboard panels, metal hangers—in various sizes and shapes—will hold most of your hand tools. For a plywood panel, metal clips—obtainable at hardware stores—will do the job.

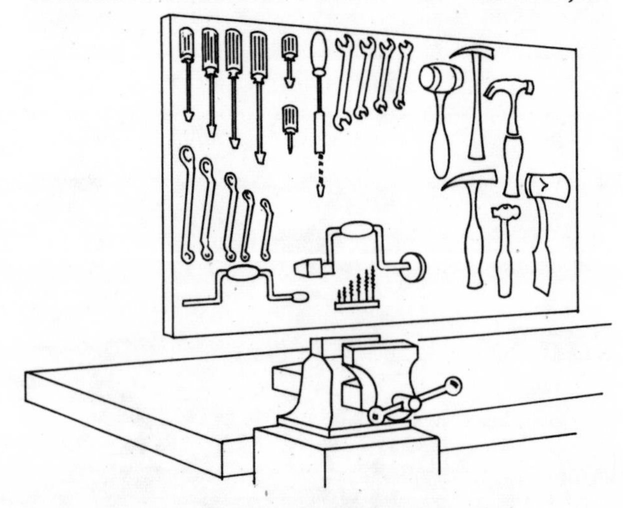

Hand tools should be hung in neat order

Of course, the cheapest method for holding tools is to use nails of assorted sizes. A small shelf fitted with slots will work for small tools such as screwdrivers and chisels. Planes can be kept on a "shelf" comprised of small dowels set into the wall panel at a slight angle.

Shallow cabinets with sturdy doors will make a triple gain for hanging tools if you're really short on space. You can hang your tools on the back panel and on both sides of the doors.

Two or more tool boards hung on a closet-door track in front of the stationary tool board is still another alternative. As tools behind each board are needed, the other boards slide out of the way.

Power tools should be movable. The ideal solution to the problem of storing large power tools (such as table or radial-arm saws) is to mount them on a movable bench or stand which is big enough to accommodate large pieces of lumber. The tool

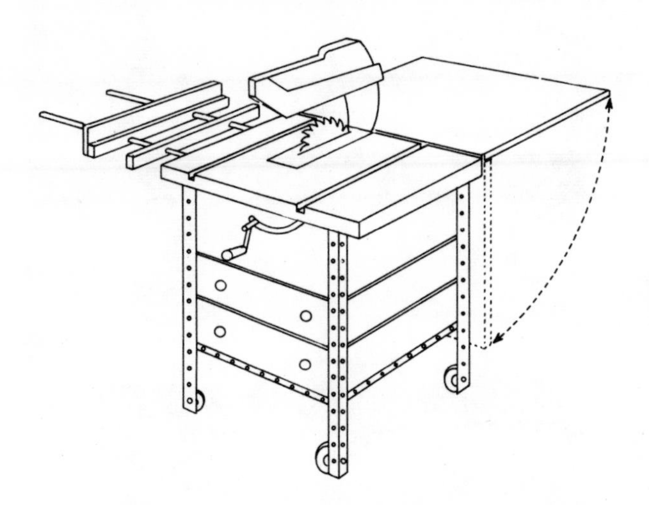

Power tools can be moved out of the way

stand can be made movable with retractable casters. Attachments can be hung on the sides of the stand, and drawers and shelving can be fitted under the mounting surface.

Keep general miscellany separate. The general miscellany of small items that collect around every workshop can also be corralled. Glass jars and tin cans have become the standard storage units for screws, bolts, and other small items. Once you have sorted out your collection, then you can search for likely storage space.

Space between studs can often be used. Simple shelves with a strip of molding to prevent containers from falling are ideal for storing small containers one-deep. For larger articles, the use of 6-inch boards as facing converts the shelves to bins.

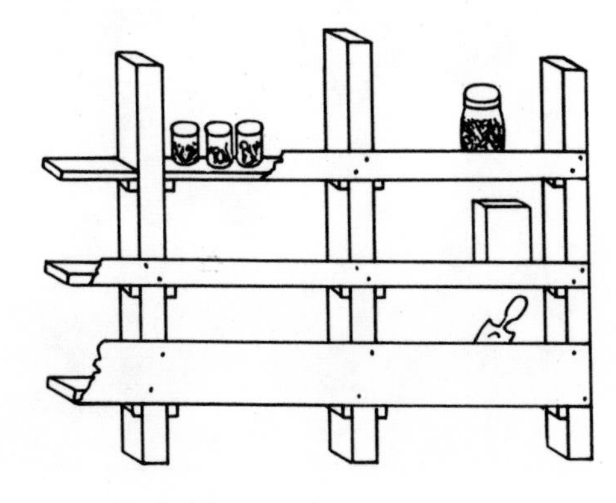

Small containers stored between studs

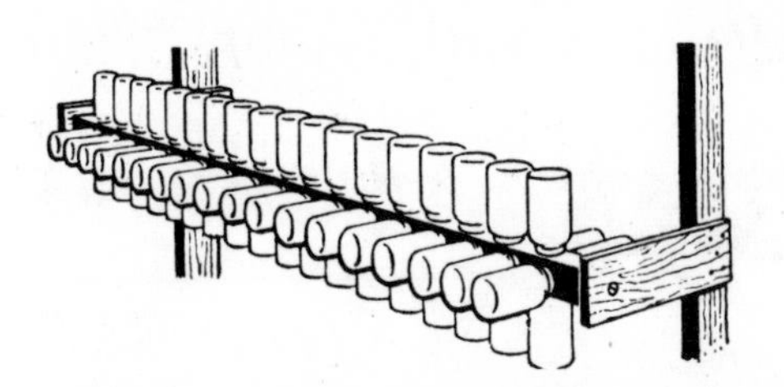

Underside of shelf for additional storage

Along the same idea, you can save space by having one set of jars on top of a shelf and nailing the lids of another set to the underside of the shelf with the jars hanging down in clear sight. Be sure to mount the jars far enough from the wall to prevent scraping of knuckles.

The area under the workbench is another location for storing miscellany. Here, varying heights of drawers and cabinets can be installed. The drawers can be swing-out or pull-out, and they may be partitioned to keep small items separated. An easy solution to partitioning drawers is to purchase plastic drawer dividers or plastic cutlery trays which will fit into the drawers.

Keep lumber off the floor

Every project done in the workshop usually has leftover scrap lumber. Some of these pieces may be big enough to be of use for another project. Also, many home handymen like to pick up lumber that is on sale, whether they need it "right now" or not. Whether scraps or brand new, this lumber requires a storage area. Here are some ideas:

Metal shelf brackets attached to wall studs will store light pieces of lumber. The brackets should be placed on every other stud. For heavier pieces of lumber, you may wish to build your own brackets. If so, scraps of wood nailed to the sides of studs will be adequate.

A sling-type steel shelf support hung from joists is an easy solution for storing long pieces of lumber.

Space between the studs for vertical stacking of lumber is another easy solution. Simple crossbars will hold smaller pieces of lumber in place.

A simple box in a dead corner will hold small scraps of lumber. This box can have a lid cut in two and joined with piano hinges to fold back. When the lid is closed, the box can serve as a temporary counter.

Large or small, workshops can be versatile and valuable

HOME WORKSHOP IS MODEST ROOM ALONGSIDE GARAGE

Cabinet with sliding doors behind multi-purpose saw holds its extra blades, buffers, sanding disks, etc. Workbench has 24 drawers holding tools, small parts; can be cleared for working with large pieces of plywood.

WORKSHOP ON SINGLE WALL OF GARAGE

Unused wall in garage contains workbench, large storage cabinets below, a pin-up board directly above for hand tools, table saw.

WORKBENCH FOR SMALL REPAIRS

Workbench has perforated hardboard walls, adjustable shelves, storage drawers below.

HOME WORKSHOP FOR LARGE PROJECTS

A workshop designed for action: Note power tools, tool rack on back wall. Arch.: Jack McAuliffe.

A DOCK-SIDE WORKSHOP

Wide doors on workshop allow for bringing boats in for work. Tool cabinet has lamp, glass jars for small items.

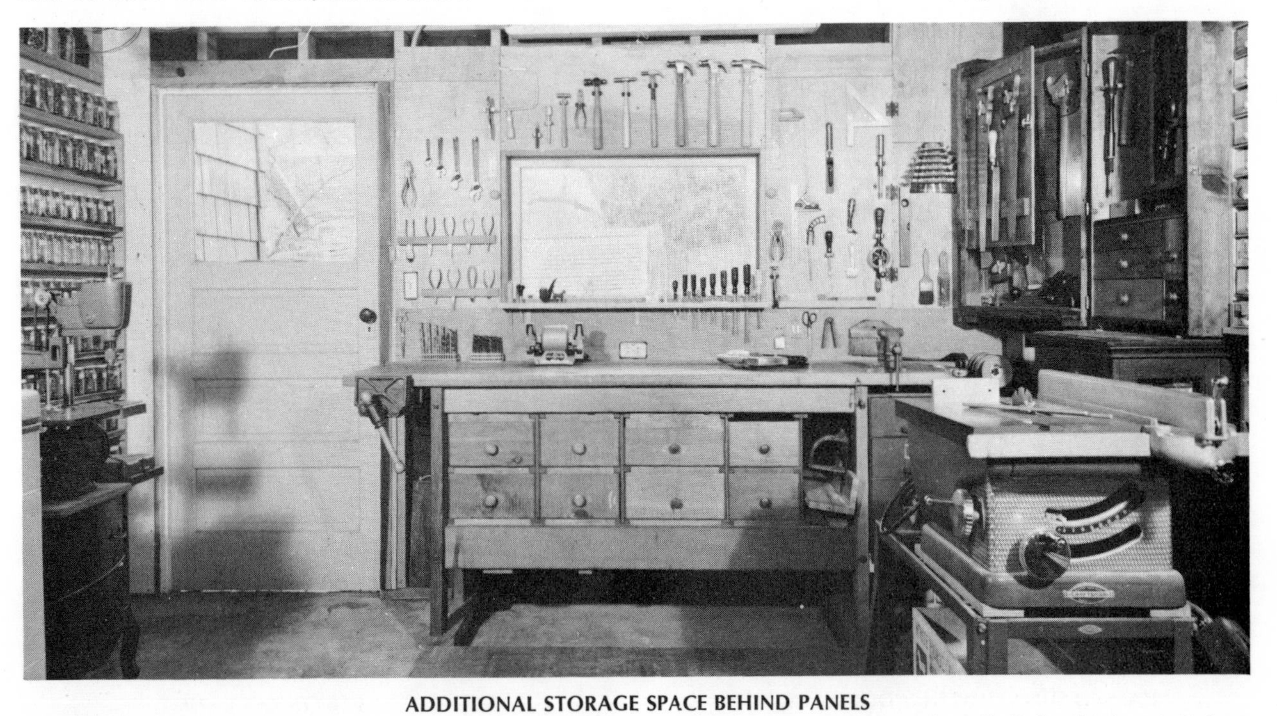

ADDITIONAL STORAGE SPACE BEHIND PANELS

Plywood panels above 7-foot workbench are hinged, swing out to reveal additional storage space behind. Workshop is roomy and well lighted (electric lights, windows both sides). Carport is beyond.

Hand tools and small parts are stored for accessibility

TOOL CABINET IS INSET A FOOT DEEP IN WALL

Holding 65 tools on brackets made of coathanger wire and metal strips, this tool cabinet is inset in a wall. Doors close to secure tool collection. Cabinet is in easy reach of workbench. Power saw swings under bench.

SLANTED SHELVES WITH WOOD DIVIDERS

Slanted shelves keep screwdrivers, chisels, drills, pliers immediately available. Small parts stored in middle.

READY TO USE ON OPEN SHELF

Drills, sanders, router store ready to use on open shelf. Note drawer with cutlery tray attached for small parts.

A portable workbench for a boy craftsman

IT ROLLS OUTDOORS FOR BIG PROJECTS

This boy's workbench is full height and roomy enough for adult use. It can be rolled out to lawn whenever a project involving mess or clutter is started. Large wheels roll over rough surfaces. Bench locks up completely.

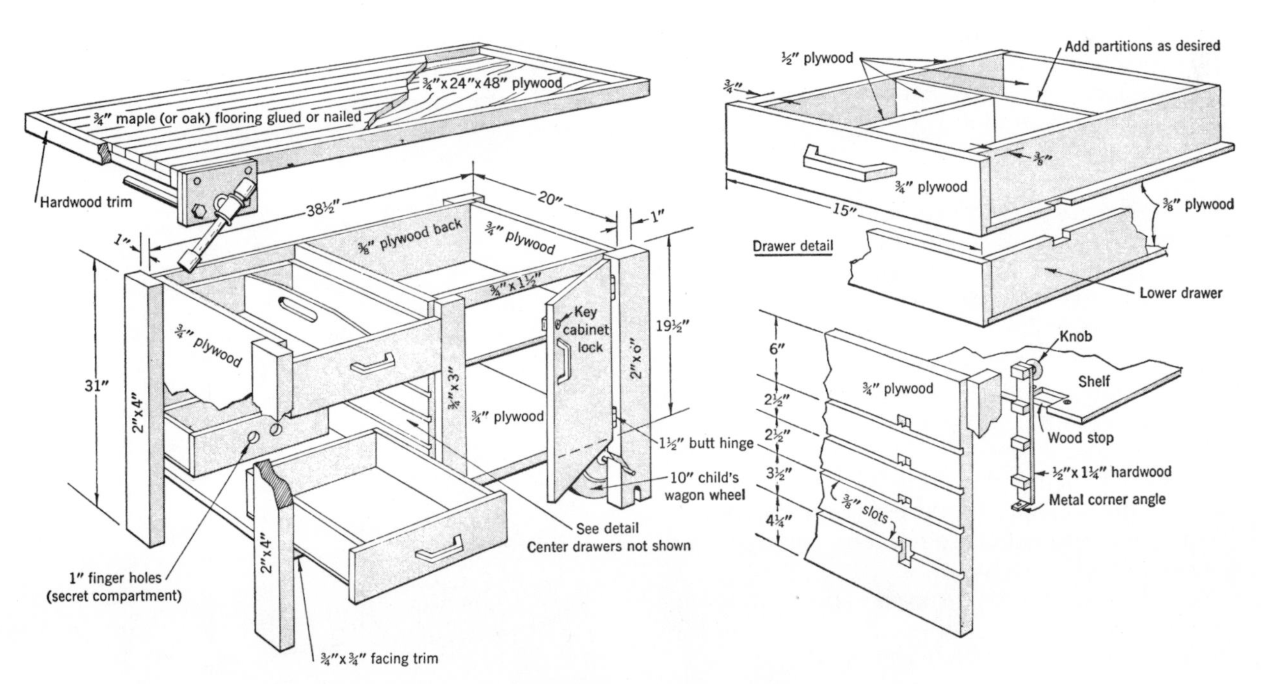

BASE CABINET IS ASSEMBLED FIRST

Assemble base cabinet first, with glue, nails, and screws. Next, the plywood top, then hardwood top. Four upper drawers are 3/8-inch "breadboards" with plywood fronts bottom drawers slide on bottom of cabinet.

Storage for

BULKY ITEMS

Storage for folding tables and chairs • Adding a closet

A storage wall in the garage • Storage space above the car

Rearranging present storage units

Lack of storage space for bulky items is a serious shortcoming of many modern-day houses. There is simply no room to store the baby buggy, bicycles, camping equipment, card tables and chairs, and the variety of bulky or heavy items that don't fit into conventional cabinets and closets.

Seldom-used items

In every home, there are items too fragile or valuable to be stored in the garage, yet too seldom used to merit large amounts of precious closet space. What do you do with the Christmas decorations, the extra bedding, the personal scrapbooks and albums, and other such items?

Re-arrange present storage units. You can often open up a few shelves or cabinets by rearranging items to make use of available space. Perhaps seldom-used items could be stored on a shelf that is too high to be reached without using a chair or stool. There may be room on the back wall of the utility room for an extra shelf, or the linen closet may have an upper shelf. Take a look in your closets. You may be surprised as to how much you can store on a shelf or in a bin without encouraging breakage.

The addition of another closet may be the only solution to gaining storage space in your home. If so, plan the closet to fit the items to be stored. A closet 24 inches deep should be adequate to handle most luggage, bedding, sporting equipment, home projection equipment, and even card tables and folding chairs.

Loose items should be stored in boxes of identical size. Boxes of the proper size can go hand-in-glove with a thoughtfully partitioned closet.

Tall pieces—such as skis and projection screens —should be set in a vertical compartment along one side of the closet.

Light objects—such as tennis rackets and ski poles—can be hung on the back wall of the closet. Items you need more often than others can be hung or put on shelves on the inside of the door.

Don't let garage be catch-all

The garage usually tends to become a catch-all for everything that is too bulky to be stored in the house. To prevent this from happening, try to set aside every square inch of space not needed for the car, the washer and dryer, or the workshop. You may be surprised to find that you have one complete wall open for storage; this wall can then be converted into a storage wall.

Organize the storage wall to fit your individual needs. You may want one section filled with sturdy shelving for canned fruit, paint cans, or other small items. A second part may be left completely open for storage of bicycles, camping equipment, or lawn furniture. A third area can be a combination

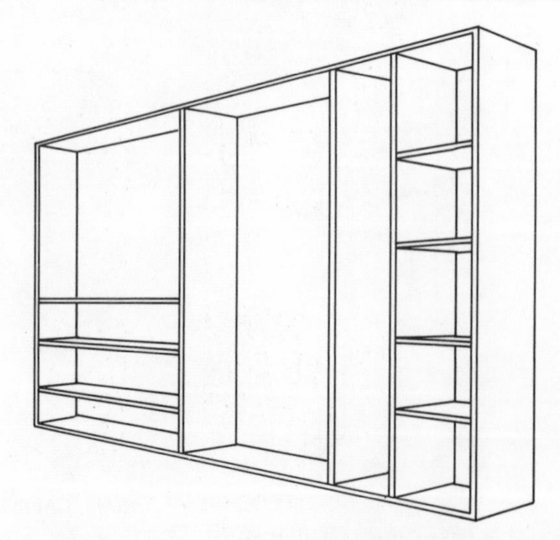

The storage wall can hold many things

of shelving and an open area to hold the croquet set, golf clubs, or small boxes.

Plan large door openings that will admit the biggest pieces you would like to store. This storage partition might just consist of 4- by 8-foot panels made into doors by the addition of hinges and hung on 3 or 4 strategically placed posts.

Space above the car may be used as an alternative to the storage wall. Whatever space is open above the car is yours for the taking, but you must allow for the garage door if it's the kind that slides overhead on a track or swings up.

Shelving suspended from the ceiling beams in the space above the car's hood can often provide the amount of storage space required.

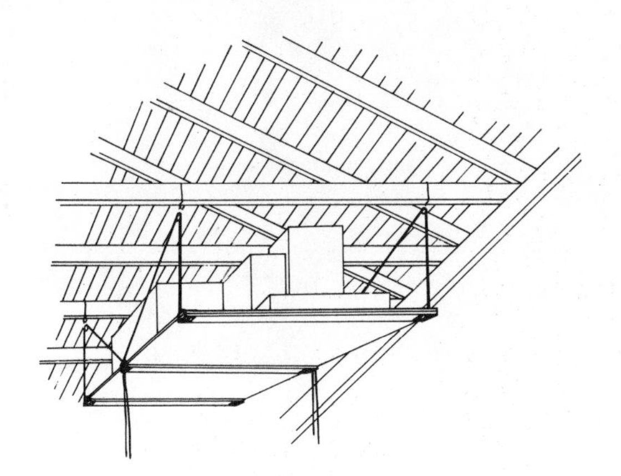

Storage above the car can be useful

A shelf operated by pulleys is a second way of using overhead space. The shelf can be located on the garage floor and then be lifted by supporting ropes run through pulleys. This method should be used only with relatively light objects that can be lifted easily. For strong support, use 1-inch-wide iron straps bent 3 inches under the shelf and screwed to bottom and sides. The cable can be attached to the ends of the straps.

Extra room may be solution

Your need for bulk storage may be so great that the only solution is an add-on to your house—either an extension of the present structure or a self-contained unit. You may be able to shorten the patio 3 or 4 feet and build a storage wall along the house. Another solution is to build a shed adjacent to the garage. Whatever solution is right for you, here are two basic requirements:

The unit should be weatherproofed, have a raised foundation, and be finished on the exterior so that it blends harmoniously with the main house and its surroundings.

Design for the future as well as the present. Make the storage unit large enough to handle bulky items you plan to acquire in the future, and try to anticipate which of your present "inventory" may be expendable in a few years.

These storage areas are partitioned for valuable items

FOR CAMERA AND RECORDING EQUIPMENT
Camera and recording equipment are stored in partitioned alcove. Arch.: William L. Fletcher.

VERTICAL STORAGE FOR FRAMED PICTURES
For vertical storage of framed pictures, shelves vary in height; are covered with carpeting to protect frames.

Folding tables and chairs occupy nooks in these homes

STAIR-STEP CLOSETS
Closets below stairs hold tables, chairs. Closed doors are barely noticeable. Design: Norman Fjeldheim.

CABINET BLENDS WITH WALL
Storage cabinet for folding tables is plywood box built into out-of-the-way corner. Archs.: Thomas and Baar.

STORAGE SPACE IS HIDDEN
Only a thin line shows when door closed. Archs.: Liebhardt & Weston.

UNUSED SPACE IN ENTRANCE HALL IS UTILIZED
This oriental style plywood cabinet in entryhall makes a handsome storage cabinet for folding tables and chairs. Design: C. H. Whitworth.

Wall space in these garages holds many things

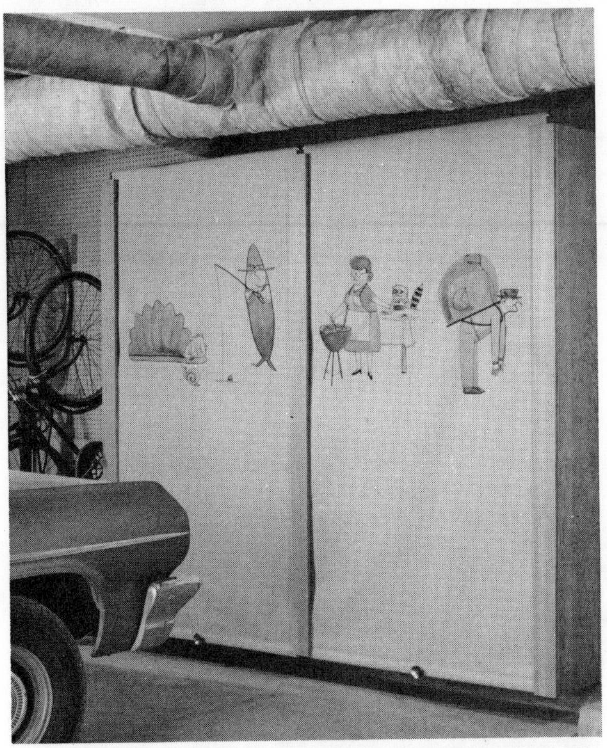

WINDOW SHADES MAKE INEXPENSIVE DOORS FOR STORAGE WALL

Two window shades close off this large garage storage cabinet. Cartoons suggest what the cabinet holds. When rolled up, shades are not in the way. Lowest shelves are adjustable, to allow for storing odd-shaped items.

DOUBLE SKI RACK

Water ski rack holds six skis side-by-side; snow ski racks holds six pairs.

BICYCLES HANG ON HOOKS

When bicycle wheel hangs on single hook, frame stands out straight.

RACKS FOR CHAISE PADS

Racks attached to garage studs are made of $2\frac{1}{2}$ by $\frac{3}{4}$-inch fir or pine.

Lofts for seldom-used items

A MINIATURE ATTIC
This 38-inch shelf for bulk storage can be constructed in garage, workshop, or hallway. Design: George Peters.

ATTIC LOFT ABOVE CAR
Sloping roof of garage creates attic space for storing boxed items and wicker furniture. Arch.: Henrik Bull.

Storage areas are added on

SEPARATE HOUSE FOR BULK STORAGE
This storage area is 6 feet deep and 25 feet long. Back wall is a concrete block wall that edges the property.

NARROW WING ADDED TO HOUSE
Addition to house provides a storage room for lumber, garden supplies. Design: Norwood and De Longe.

Carports provide storage

BIKE BIN AND GARDEN STORAGE
Anchored between two posts of carport, storage bin holds garden pots, bicycles. Archs.: Terry and Moore.

STORAGE WALL DIVIDED INTO COMPARTMENTS
One side of carport forms divided storage wall for garden supplies, building supplies. Arch.: Lutah Maria Riggs.

SERVES AS DIVIDER AND STORAGE ROOM
Also serving as divider between carport and entry walk, 4 by 6½-foot structure has shelves for suitcases, trunks, car washing equipment. Tools hang on back wall. Door opens on entry walk side. Design: Neil Crawford.

Storage for

GARDEN TOOLS, SUPPLIES

A work-storage center • Possible location sites • Local zoning ordinances

Design for easy access • Hanging long-handled implements

A compact potting bench • Storing bulky materials

It is the tendency of most gardeners to keep all tools and supplies, and then to add new ones as intriguing innovations appear on the market. This habit presents a continuous storage problem.

Establish a work-storage center

The primary purpose of a combination work-storage unit is to keep equipment and supplies easily at hand. But it can also prove useful as a screen to an unsightly scene—or fit into a narrow area otherwise not suited for use—or become a part of an already existing outdoor structure.

Prefabricated storage units are available in varying sizes and shapes. These units provide adequate shelter for tools and supplies, but the interiors are not always equipped with drawers and bins or with devices for keeping hand tools separate from power tools. You may prefer to purchase the outside shell and design and build the interior according to your needs. Or it may be more practical for you to build the whole structure. Either way, here are two basic considerations:

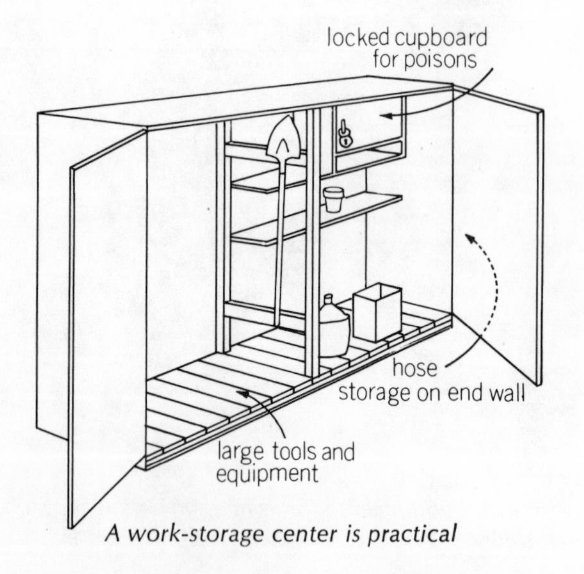

A work-storage center is practical

Proximity to the garden. Actually, the size and shape of your lot can be the deciding factor (despite your personal desires) to possible location sites. "The garden" is quite often two gardens (front and back), or even four gardens if you grow things along the sides of your house. If you have a choice as to where to store garden equipment and can't make up your mind, remember that it is a real advantage to have the storage area close to a driveway. Bales of peat moss, sacks of fertilizer, or other bulky items that you bring back from the nursery in your car can be tough on the lifting muscles.

Generally speaking, a sensible solution is to locate the garden work center at the side of the house and not too far from the garage. Other possible locations are against a back fence, adjacent to the patio, next to the garage, or in a back corner of your lot. In the latter case, the storage unit could be hidden by a simple fence or shrubbery.

An obvious solution often overlooked: Have *two* storage locations, one (in the garage) for bulky or seldom-used items, the other (wherever most convenient) for items used most frequently.

Check with local zoning ordinances before actually placing a prefabricated storage unit or before you begin constructing one. Some local zoning ordinances specify exactly how close to a side or rear yard fence these units can be placed. In many locations you can put a structure anywhere you want as long as it isn't anchored to the ground or a concrete slab. In other areas you may find that you must abide by requirements governing detached structures in side or rear yards.

Design for easy access

When planning storage for garden implements, allow for easy access. Whether the storage unit is a walk-in or a small shelter, keep sills low so there will be no trouble removing wheeled implements. Also, make doors wide enough to clear the broadest lawn mower or garden cart. Here are some other important features to consider.

Hang long-handled implements. The longest rakes and hoes can be hung vertically or horizontally in a storage unit 6 feet high and 6 feet wide. Hooks or brackets do the job, leaving the floor area clear for bulky implements, sacks, and boxes.

Store bulky materials such as fertilizers and soil mixing materials (peat moss, leaf mold, etc.) in enclosed cabinets or boxes to keep moisture out and dryness in where needed.

A garbage can — plastic or metal — can be mounted on racks. Material is easily shoveled out of the can without removing it from its place.

Garbage cans store bulky material

Another way to use garbage cans is to attach them to caster-mounted dollies. This works particularly well if the storage center has a concrete floor.

Pull-out bins also serve as convenient containers for loose materials. The size of the bins can be modified to fit available space, but the most convenient spot is under a work bench. Here, the bins

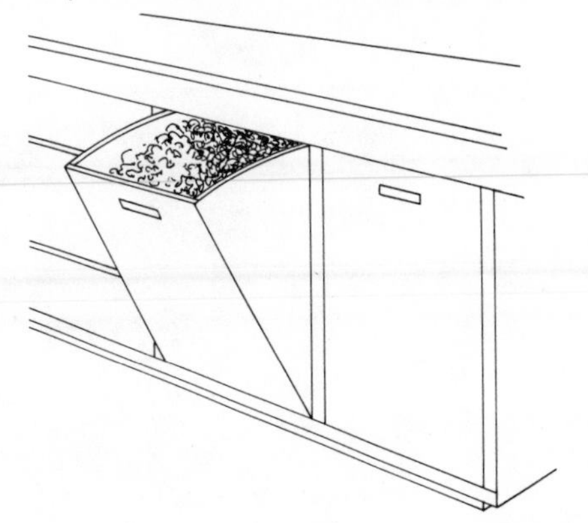

Pull-out bins for loose materials

can be used in place or pulled out when they are nearly empty. Partitioning of each bin will allow for storing of two different types of material.

Keep poisons under lock and key. For anyone who uses chemicals for pest and disease control—and this applies especially to families with small children—a storage box with a lock and key is a must. Inexpensive wood or metal boxes can be bolted to a wall out of a child's reach. It is best to keep this storage box in the garage or some other sheltered place besides the house itself.

The jog in this fence is a roomy garden storage shed

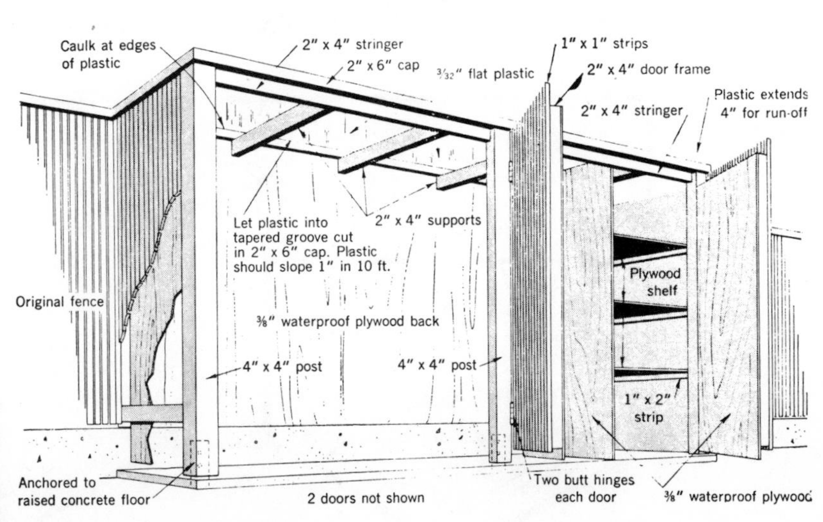

STORAGE SHED BLENDS WITH FENCE

Long, thin shed (10 feet long, 3 feet wide) fits between fence and walk. Open door reveals plastic top, shelves, plywood inner paneling. Siding and plastic top supported by 2 by 2's. Landscape Arch.: Robert Chitock.

Here is an all-purpose garden storage unit

IT'S NEAT LOOKING AND MOVABLE

The four doors of this shed open wide—anything, everything is accessible. Raised floor helps keep shed dry, has ramp for wheelbarrow, lawnmower. Potting counter includes three bins below for bulky peat moss, mulches.

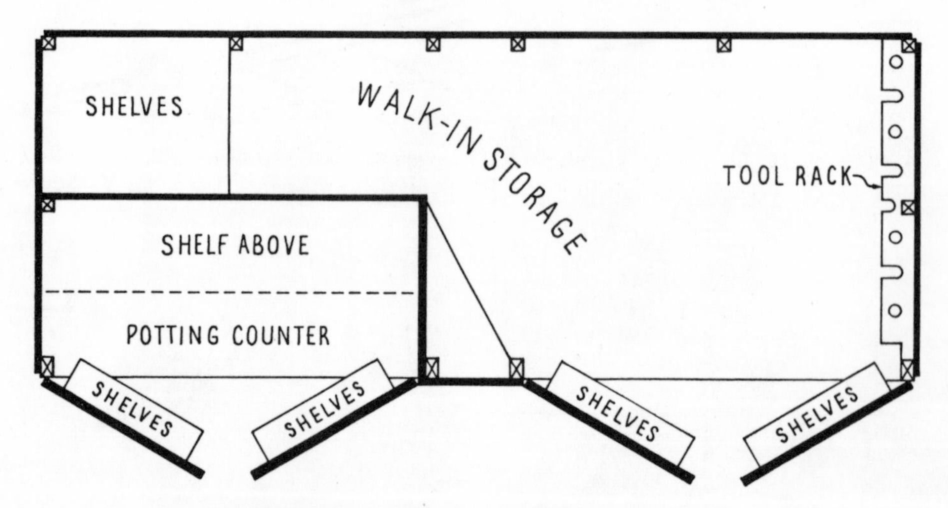

FLOOR PLAN SHOWS ECONOMY OF SPACE

Shed's floor plan shows economy and simplification of 3½ by 9-foot size. There is space behind potting counter for off-season storage of sports and camping equipment. Door shelves make use of that ordinarily wasted space.

DRAWERS TILT DOWNWARD
Two outer drawers automatically tilt downward when pulled out. Sliding gate regulates, stops flow of material.

BIN FRONT HINGES DOWN FOR FILLING
Upper half of bin front hinges down for filling and for easy access when bin's contents are inconveniently low.

SHELF RESTS ON PERFORATED HARDBOARD
Adjustable upper shelf for extra pots and containers rests on perforated hardboard brackets, tools on similar hooks.

NOTCHED BOARD HOLDS TOOLS
Tool rack is a notched board with pieces of plastic garden hose nailed to the edge; tools are stored upright.

Storage center worth study

AT FIRST GLANCE, IT LOOKS LIKE CHILD'S PLAYHOUSE

Tiny work center is simple wooden frame structure with a brick floor, corrugated plastic roof, a lath overhang in front. Garden tools, fertilizers, sprays are stored on one side; other side has a potting bench, shelves.

Cabinets provide storage

MODULAR BOXES NESTLED UNDER EAVES

Simple cabinets make handy garden storage and work center. Hung horizontally, they provide counter top (picture at right has counter top made of 3/4-inch plywood covered with 1/8-inch hardboard).

A compact potting bench

25¼"
4"
4" STRAP HINGE
1"x6" T&G REDWOOD
1"
33½"
28"
2"x 2" REDWOOD
PLASTIC CONTAINER
10"

30¾"
1¾"
1"x 4" CLEATS
13"
13"
1"x4" FIR DRAWER GUIDES
¾" EXTERIOR PLYWOOD DRAWER - SEE DETAIL A
26½"
2"
12"
1"x1"
10" DIA.
4½"
DETAIL A - PLAN VIEW

FOR THE AVERAGE-SIZED HOME GARDEN

Four gaily colored plastic pails, dropped through holes in pull-out shelves, contain peat moss; leaf mold, sand.

End view shows simple construction; shelf can be added on lower support. Half-view shows pails suspended.

Every tool has a place

RACK CAN BE MODIFIED FOR SMALL TOOLS

This tool storage rack is made of 2 by 8 with holes 2 inches in diameter drilled at an angle toward the base.

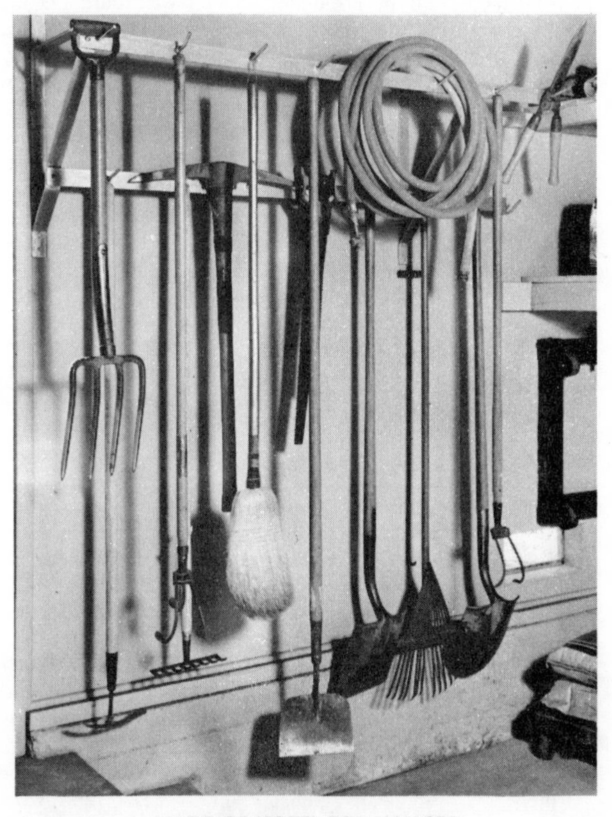

MADE OF HOTEL POT HANGER

Tool rack is mounted high on garage wall to keep floor clear. Screw eyes in ends of handles slip over hooks.

CONSTRUCTION HINTS

Selecting and installing units

After you have designed the storage needed, you have the choice of buying or building the units. If you lack adequate tools in your home workshop or are not inclined toward woodworking, you may prefer to buy prefabricated cabinets.

You can save some money and use your own construction procedures on factory-made units if you buy them precut and machined, but not assembled. Cabinets in most stock sizes are available in this form; you purchase a kit containing all the parts, cut and sanded, and all the necessary nails, glue, screws, hardware, and instructions for construction and finishing.

If you find that standard units do not fit your needs, and are not equipped to construct your own cases, you may want to have your units custom made. This, of course, is the most expensive method of adding storage space, but there are compensations. You can order any size units, tailored to meet your specific needs, with counter tops at preferred heights and storage space divided into cabinets, drawers, or bins and faced with any hardwood that suits you.

If you order custom cabinets directly from a shop, without a remodeling or building contractor, you may have to hang doors, attach hinges and hardware, finish the units, and install them yourself.

Steel Units

Standard steel cabinets are available to fit corners, form round ends of kitchen peninsulas, and provide for ranges or sinks that jut out from the wall. In both wall and base cabinets, you can obtain adjustable shelves, sliding shelves, pull-out trays, bins of all kinds, drawers, and even a fold-out desk for the kitchen. Special drawer and tray dividers for storage of silver, fruits and vegetables, bulk flour and sugar, trays, linens, and kitchen utensils are obtainable. Special reinforced shelves for storage of heavy case lots or bulk packages can be fitted into standard units.

Custom steel kitchens are available, if stock sizes do not fit your needs. These kitchens are designed and then constructed at the manufacturer's plant; no construction work is done at your home.

Steel cabinets come in standard sizes that fit almost all kitchens. Wall cabinets are obtainable in widths from 12 to 36 inches, by 3 or 4-inch increments; combination units come up to 66 inches wide, and special cabinets may be as narrow as 6 inches. Heights range from 12 to 30 inches, with 24 and 30 the most common. Depths are standardized at 13 inches, with some specialty cabinets and half-cabinets only 5 inches deep.

Base cabinet widths are the same as wall units; heights are set at either 34³/₄ or 34¹/₂ inches; with addition of a counter top, this brings the unit to a 36-inch height. Depths are set at 24¹/₂ or 25 inches, providing adequate counter top.

Utility cabinets are 64 to 84 inches high, 24 to 30 inches wide, and 13 to 25 inches deep. This size cabinet is designed to hold cleaning implements or, if fitted with shelves, miscellaneous storage.

Wood Units

The workability of wood and its adaptability to any kind of interior decor make wood storage units popular and widely-used throughout the home. Wood built-ins and free-standing units to meet all storage needs can either be purchased in stock sizes or be custom-made.

Single cases cover a wide range of sizes. Wall cabinets are from 12 to 30 inches high, and vary from 8 to 36 inches in width. Depth for all but half-cabinets is 12 inches. Cabinets to fit over refrigerators or range hoods are stock, as are spice shelves and corner units. Kitchen base cabinets are 24 to 26 inches deep, 34 to 35 inches high, and equal in width to the wall cabinets.

For the bedroom, there are ready-made wardrobe closets, vanities, dressers, chests of drawers, shoe racks, open shelf units, and cabinets. These cases may be combined in a single frame to form a storage wall, or they may be used individually as built-ins or free-standing conveniences.

The same type of adaptations can be used for a music wall, buffet storage, desks, and family room storage walls. By purchasing units of equal depth, and in modular heights and widths, any combination of cabinets, drawers, and open shelving can be arranged to form a storage wall.

Installing Wall Cabinets

Wall cabinets may be installed on hanger bars, furring strips, or directly to the wall studs. Some manufacturers of metal units provide a hanger bar; this is screwed into the wall studs at a specified height and the cabinets have notches that fit on the bar.

Furring strips are good for both wood and steel cabinets. The furring serves double duty: To give a level nailing piece on which to fasten the cabinets, and to compensate for any unevenness in the back wall. If wood cabinets have a nailing piece built-in, furring is not needed unless the wall is uneven. By inserting shims behind the furring strip, a level base for installing the cabinets is formed. When you attach furring for metal units, align it with the two sets of cabinet-to-wall anchor holes in the cabinet backs to eliminate drilling new holes. Three-inch boards, ³/₄-inch thick, are commonly used for furring.

If the cabinets have recessed backs, furring and hanger bars will be covered after the units are hung. But with flush backs, extend the furring to the cabinet edges; later, it can both support and be covered by molding.

If the cabinets have flush backs, the back piece is firmly nailed to the side panels, and the room wall is level and sound, there may be no need for furring.

When the cabinets are lifted into place, nail them temporarily to the furring or wall studs; then check for level. If no furring is used, you may have to insert shims behind the units to compensate for uneven spots in the wall. When the cabinets are in place, either nail or screw them securely into the back wall. Secure the connecting bolts, add molding if needed, and the job is finished.

Installing Base Cabinets

The same procedure used for wall cabinets can be applied to base units; the installation is somewhat simplified since you can arrange the cabinets in place on the floor without lifting and juggling.

When installing new cases over an old wall, clear the wall surface of trim and molding to provide a snug fit. Arrange the cabinets against the wall, working from the corner, and check for level. If the floor is uneven, slip shim under corners of the cabinet base; do the same behind the cabinet backs or furring to straighten any wall defects. If fillers are used, line them up with wall cabinet fillers to give proper balance.

Some wood cabinets are purchased without integral bases. If so, construct a base of 3/4-inch stock, from the back wall to 3 inches from the cabinet facing; this indentation gives proper toe room. Most

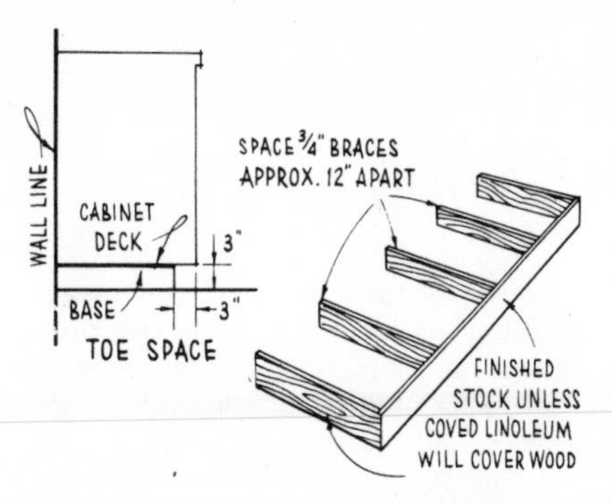

bases are 3 inches high, but you can adjust this to either lower or raise the counter top.

Base cabinets can be purchased either with or without counter tops. If installing a single unit, a built-on top will save you time and trouble. But with a series of cabinets, a continuous work surface without joints is usually preferred, so cabinets without built-on tops should be obtained.

Installing Closets

Units larger than wall and base cabinets will stand on their own feet, but only until they are loaded. To keep closets from pulling away from the wall or actually toppling over, you can anchor them in the same way as the smaller cabinets. Since the structure of closets is stronger, you may not need furring if the back wall is level. Nails or screws driven in the wall studs will in most cases hold the large units in place.

Installing shelves or other storage units in the kitchen, utility room, garage, or carport may involve attaching brackets or cabinets to masonry walls. To do this, you need a drill hard enough to penetrate masonry, and special anchoring devices to hold the screws or nails that do the fastening.

An electric hand drill with carbide-tip bit is one of the most efficient tools for drilling in masonry. If you don't own a drill, you can either rent one or use a star drill and hammer—tools requiring more patience but quite capable of getting the job done.

To plug the holes, you can choose from several types of low cost anchors designed for use in masonry. All work on the same principle: They expand against the side of the holes in the masonry as nails or screws are inserted in them. Plugs are available in plastic, wood, or metal; the outside diameter of the plug should equal size of bit used to drill.

Counter tops

Home owners who install new base cabinets in kitchen, bath, or utility room will find it necessary to select a counter top to both cover the cabinets and form a work surface. The kitchen counter merits the most attention, since this will receive constant use. There are several types of counter tops available, and the best surface for your home will depend on style of the room, and your ability as a home craftsman.

Metal, tile, wood, linoleum, and plastic coverings are available, in a wide range of prices and styles. Stainless steel, ceramic tile, and rigid laminated plastic are the most popular counter materials, both for appearance and usefulness. Linoleum and wood require repeated care to maintain their appearance, and neither can withstand acid, heat and abuse as well as other surfaces.

Stainless steel counters are neat, shiny, easy to keep clean, tough, and permanent. But stainless steel will not totally resist acids, ink, and other chemicals, and a reasonable amount of care in keeping the surface clean is necessary to prevent stains. Metal counters also are not for the home craftsman, since they must be custom made in a sheet metal shop at a relatively high cost.

Ceramic tile has long been the standard kitchen and bath counter material because it is durable, resists dents, stains, and scratches, and its finish is baked in and requires no maintenance. The skilled home craftsman can set tile, but a professional is usually required on most jobs. The cost per square foot is less than steel, and about equal to a professional installation of plastic.

Rigid laminated plastics have become popular because of the non-porous, hard surface, little maintenance required, and resistance to acids, heat, and alkalies. Plastic is more expensive than linoleum and some woods, but is less costly than metal. For a custom kitchen with coved or contoured backs and "dripless" edges, professional shop work is required. But the fairly experienced home craftsman

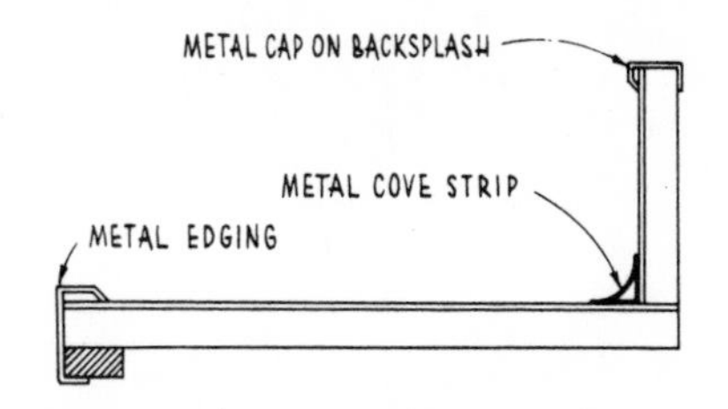

can install a plastic counter if the job involves only flat surfaces, with metal edging and cove strips used at joints.

The usefulness of plastic laminates has prompted manufacturers to produce package counter tops, cut to fit the individual kitchen and mounted on plywood or metal, ready to install on the base cabinets. This type of counter may be best for your kitchen, if you have not done any previous work with plastics.

Hinged doors

Hinged doors have long been the standard for cabinets and closets, withstanding the attack of sliding and folding units and still holding up as the best type door for many storage cases.

The main advantage of swinging doors is that the entire closet or cabinet is opened with one movement. There are no tracks, ridges, or guides to collect dust and mar appearance, and the storage unit interior may be altered in many ways without removing or replacing the doors.

Cabinet and closet doors can be either flush or lip. Flush doors may be desirable to give a uniform appearance to a series of units, or for ease of installation with butt hinges; they also can be recessed or attached so they project slightly.

Flush doors are not popular with some craftsmen because they amplify any errors; when the house or cabinets settle, or hinges begin to sag, flush doors magnify the problem by either jamming against the cabinet frame or showing an open space along the door edges.

Doors are available in standard sizes from builders' supply houses; they come in a variety of facings and styles. If stock units will not fit your cabinets, either have them cut at a cabinet shop or make them yourself to match the cabinet frames.

Hinges in many ways determine the success of the door; use hinges that will support the full weight of the door and are strong enough to open and close easily without sagging or sticking. The variety of styles and finishes available enables you to purchase hinges that either enhance the beauty of the cabinet work or are completely concealed when the door is closed. A few extra dollars invested on hinges for often-used cabinets will eliminate troubles and forego replacement within a short time.

Latches also are important to the success or failure of swinging doors. There are several different types and styles on the market, each featuring a different "trap." When selecting catches, keep in mind the amount of work it will be required to do; solid types that are not likely to loosen or bend, and are not dependent on strict alignment to function properly are best for cabinets and closets subject to constant use.

When hanging doors, allow for freedom of movement both between paired doors and around hinges. Some carpenters judge the amount of space needed between matching doors by inserting a paper match between them and then setting hinges. This clearance allows for free movement and prevents the doors from sticking together.

Sliding doors

Sliding doors on cabinets and closets offer a number of advantages over hinged doors. They may be quickly moved aside, take up minimum space, offer a clean, attractive surface, and—on better hardware—roll along quietly, without much of a push.

The main disadvantage of sliding doors is that only half the cabinet or closet can be opened at once when overlapping doors are used. This can be troublesome when two people are trying to use the same wardrobe closet at the same time, or large objects must be maneuvered in and out of a cabinet.

For small wall cabinets, a simple and inexpensive sliding door can be made of 1/8-inch or 1/4-inch tempered hardboard, or 1/4-inch plywood. You can use 1/4-inch round as guides, and cut panels to fit the opening with a 1/16-inch clearance for easy sliding. For overlapping doors, use a 1/4-inch-square strip in the center and round for the sides. Sand the edges of the panels and soap the slots.

With new units you can rabbet the channels in the shelves. A good channel depth for 3/4-inch shelving is 1/2" at top, 1/4" at bottom, so you can lift the door up into the upper channel to remove it.

Double channels can be used for sliding doors. The bottom of this channel is curved up to provide a minimum of bearing surface and give an easy movement. At the top of the door, use the same channels, inverted, or use rabbeted grooves; with the channels, add wood stops to give enough depth for removal of the shelves.

Rolling doors

Rolling doors are designed for larger closets and wardrobes where weight of the door causes bowing and too much friction on channels and runners. Rolling doors hang from the top of the opening on flanged tracks, attached by a hanger with a roller wheel to fit in the track, and held in place with guides for the bottom of the door. Ball-bearing nylon wheels, the most expensive type, are also the most efficient.

Tracks are available to fit doors from 5/8-inch to 1 3/8 inches thick. You may buy kits including all necessary hardware, screws, and directions.

The door can be of 5/8-inch or 3/4-inch plywood, for smaller cabinets and storage walls, or you can use hollow-core or lumber-core doors 1 3/8 inches thick for larger installations.

Guides for the door bottoms vary, but all serve the same purpose of keeping the door steady and providing a positive action. The top roller hangers are installed on the back sides of the doors, with 1/4-inch clearance off the floor; the guides are placed so the door is channeled in a straight line. The screw type is the most common, but requires that a channel be rabbeted in the bottom of the door. A more expensive guide has a floor plate and runner that screws to the back of the door and needs no rabbet.

Folding doors

Folding doors combine the best features of both hinged and sliding doors; they are stored in the opening they create, and still open up the entire closet or cabinet at once. Stock doors are available in heights from 6'8" to 13 feet, and will span any width from 2 feet to 30 feet.

All folding doors operate on the same principle: The door is hung on tracks or pivots on the top of the doorway, and is hinged to one side of the opening and latched to the other. When opened, the door folds on itself and forms a "stack" at the hinged end.

Folding doors are available in steel, wood, plastic, and natural fabrics. There are three general types: pantograph, hinged panels, and folding wood slats. For doors that have curves or angles, the pantograph is best, since it can be rounded in fluid rather than rigid shapes.

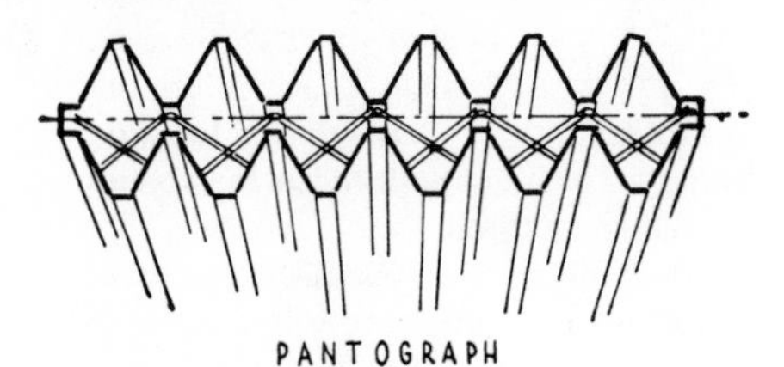

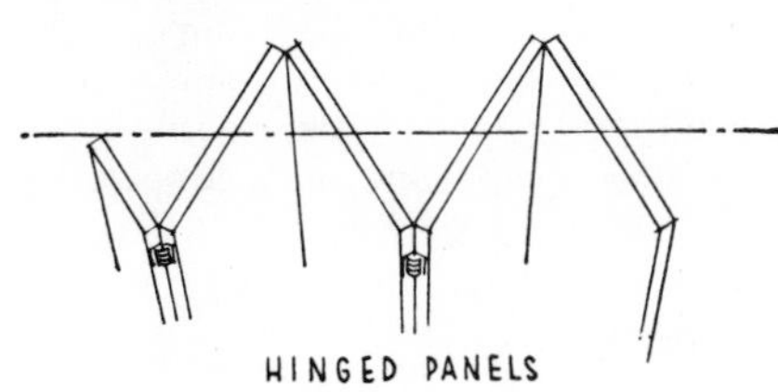

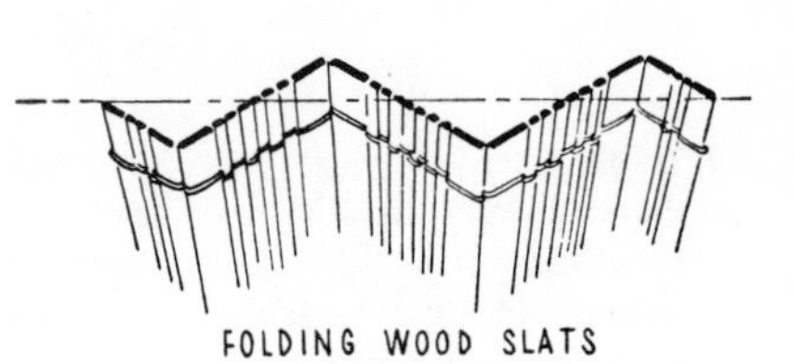

Cabinet interiors

The most important element in designing storage units to fit your needs is how the unit interiors are arranged. Whether you are buying or building new cases, or altering those already installed, plan to include every possible convenience to increase the efficiency of the units and eliminate waste space.

Many times, you will find that construction can be simplified by the use of special hardware pieces and mechanical devices available. When struggling with a particular problem, go to a good hardware or builders' supply store and look over the specialty pieces; if you don't find exactly what you want, explain your problem to a salesman. If he is familiar with wholesale sources and has sold to professional cabinet makers, he probably has in stock or can order the exact gadget or piece of equipment you need. The number and type of these specialties is constantly increasing and it would be worth the time and effort to become familiar with all of them.

Stationary Shelves

Stationary shelving shows up in almost every storage unit, supporting all types of articles and at times forming a structural part of the unit. The size and type wood used varies greatly, depending on the desired appearance and the load to be supported. Methods of shelf support are standardized, but are open to variation and combination to gain additional support.

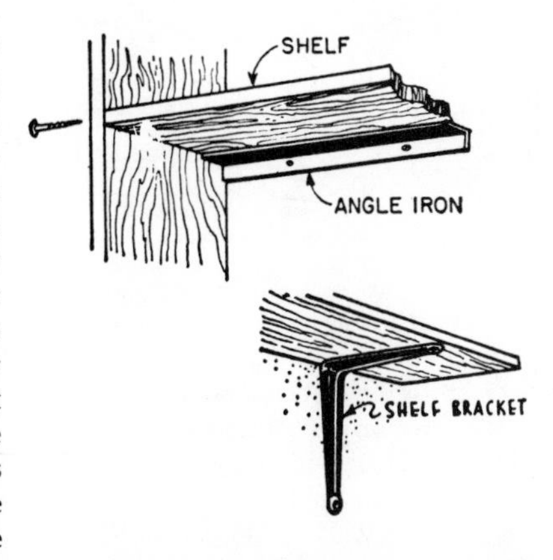

Metal brackets, braces, and angle irons can be purchased in a wide variety of sizes, shapes, and styles for attaching open shelves.

With long shelving, such as in a bookcase, it may be necessary to give added strength by using upright wood supports at the span's midpoint or spaced at one or two-foot intervals; by setting the vertical braces against the back wall, they are less noticeable than a flush installation and still provide the needed support.

Adjustable Shelving

Adjustable shelving many times is the best method of eliminating waste space in storage units. By adjusting the shelf heights to fit the items stored, you can add an appreciable amount of new storage space without altering the basic structure of the case.

When planning to use adjustable shelves, keep in mind the clearances needed to remove any of the articles stored on the shelves. Even with one-deep storage, an inch or two over the tallest article is needed to remove everything on the shelf; with deeper storage, the clearances needed increase proportionately. Also note that adjustable shelves are not attached to supports, and only rest on top of brackets; uneven loading or careless handling may cause a wobbly shelf or one that tilts. If the articles stored are breakable, be sure the brackets are securely fastened to standards or are firmly inserted in the wall.

The units consist of a metal strip approximately 5/8-inch wide that is installed on the wall surface. Accompanying brackets that serve as the shelf rests can be inserted snugly anywhere on the strip. For end support, a pair of standards and two brackets are needed for each wall; with back supports, one pair of wall strips should do, unless the shelves are extra long. Stock lengths of the standards range from 24 to 144 inches. Brackets snap into place.

For shelves that threaten to tip, set inverted brackets above the shelf to form a "grip" on the shelf and hold it in place.

Special Shelves

There are two types of special shelving that deserve consideration because of their usefulness: Half-shelves and door shelves. Both types are used to gain additional storage space in a closet or cabinet without altering the over-all dimensions of the unit.

Half-shelves are usually found in kitchen cabinets and in storage units for dinnerware, but are useful in any storage center where waste space between stationary shelves is a problem. A half-shelf is nothing more than a miniature bench, made of 1/4 or 1/2-inch plywood. The bench should be full width of the cabinet, but only half the height and half the depth of regular shelf openings.

Factory-made units of this type are common; you can purchase either wood or metal "cages" and shelves up to five or six inches deep, to fit any door.

Sliding Shelves and Trays

Sliding shelves and trays are basically the same thing. A tray is usually nothing more than a sliding shelf with sideboards, front, and back added. They both serve the same general purpose . . . to make items stored in deep cabinets easily accessible without wasting space.

To support sliding shelves, you can obtain a pair of metal shelf guides that are attached to cabinet sides and provide an outside track for the shelf. You may prefer to install wooden rails above and below the shelf for a guide, but the principle of operation remains the same. When installing the guides and cutting shelves, leave room for closing the cabinet or closet door.

There are several ways to make wood shelf guides. The easiest is to nail strips on the cabinet walls for top and bottom guides. For shelves to be heavily loaded, you can use metal angle irons which form a 5/8-inch shelf to support the tray; the

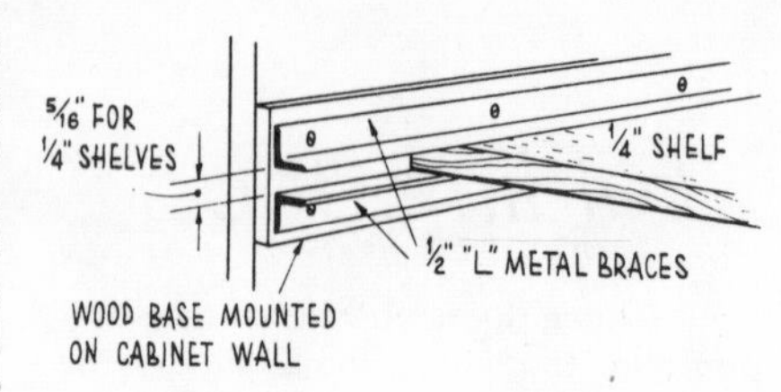

top guide is as necessary as the bottom, since this will receive the stress when the shelf is pulled out and begins to sag with its own weight.

For normal loads, such as clothes or dishes, 3/8-inch plywood shelves are strong enough; 1/2-inch is best for heavy loads, and 5/8-inch plywood is needed for very heavy items, such as books or phonograph records.

Pop-ups

Pop-up shelves are useful in the kitchen for storing appliances, in a desk to accommodate a typewriter, or in a sewing center for storage of a sewing machine. In all cases, the operation is the same: The machine or appliance is permanently stored on a shelf that is raised and lowered on metal hardware that eliminates lifting and carrying the machine from point of storage to point of use.

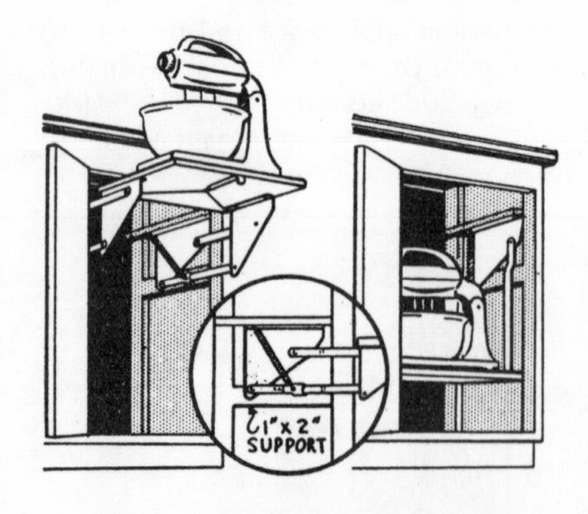

Hardware for such an installation can be purchased to fit any cabinet opening; the only requirement is at least 23 inches of height for the machine, shelf on which it sits, hardware, and clearance for movement of the entire assembly. You can obtain hardware that fits directly under the counter top, or a different set that is mounted lower in the cabinet door and permits installation of a drawer between cabinet and counter top.

The amount of space needed for a pop-up dictates that it be used scrupulously; the unit will waste space unless the entire height needed for the swinging mechanism is used for storing a tall object.

Drawers

The drawer is one of the most popular and useful of all storage units. Because every item stored in the unit can be pulled into sight and within easy reach.

Drawers are available in stock sizes, can be custom made to fit your particular needs, or can be constructed in the home workshop. The major disadvantage of drawers is the difficulty in building solid, trouble-free units; professional cabinet makers regard them as among the most difficult tasks, and home craftsmen will regard them in equal light after considering the cutting, grooving, fitting, and special joints needed.

Molded plastic drawers can be used either as separate built-ins or fitted individually in a wood unit.

The drawers come complete and ready to install; they are more expensive than wood units of equal sizes, but this may be compensated by the time and labor saved. The drawers need no sanding or finishing, have round corners to eliminate dust, are easily cleaned, don't warp or stick, and resist chipping and cracking.

Single drawers vary in width from 16 to 34 1/2 inches, in several depths. Bottom drawer guides and outside top hanger rails are molded in, and the drawers are installed on wood supports for the rails or on a bottom runner to fit the molded guide. Drawer fronts can be left in natural plastic, painted, or covered with a plywood facing.

Metal drawers are available in full counter-height units, or as singles that can be installed as substitutes for any wood drawer of equal size. Each drawer hangs and slides from its own lid, which is fastened to the cabinet frame; the lids can be installed for either flush or lipped drawers.

To add them to old cabinets, all cleats, shelves, or old drawer supports are removed. Two center rails are placed over the drawer opening, in line with the prebored holes of the lid. The lid is then

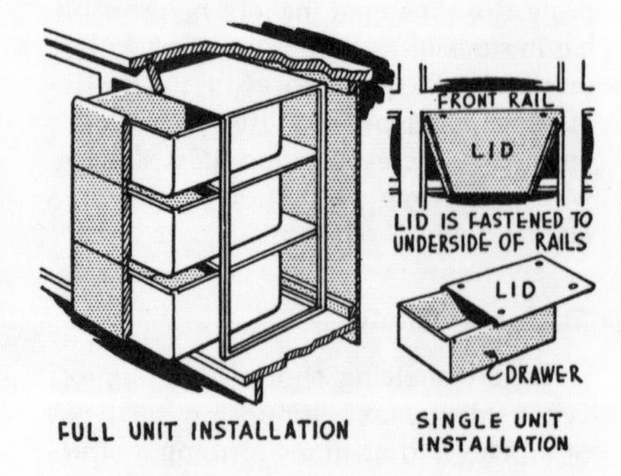

screwed to the rails, either flush or inset 3/4-inch, depending on whether flush or lip fronts are desired. The drawer is fitted with the wood front and inserted in the opening, sliding on the guides built in the lid. If needed, 3/4-inch face rails can be placed between each drawer, glued and nailed to the old face frame. The center lid supports can be nailed to these and the back cabinet wall.

Wood drawers can be bought or built, according to your woodworking talents and complexity of the storage unit.

If stock units are satisfactory, a variety of sizes and styles are available, either in singles or stacks of two, three, or four. Single drawers, pre-cut but unassembled, can be purchased for installation in new cabinets or in old units.

Complete drawer units also are available, ranging from the ordinary unfinished chest for family room or bedroom, to 15-inch-wide kitchen series, complete with toe base.

If stock sizes don't fit your storage plan or can't be set in old cabinets you want to continue using, the only solution may be to have the drawers custom made. When ordering drawers, be prepared to tell the cabinet maker the size and depth of the drawer opening, the type front material wanted, whether the front will be flush or lipped, if front rails will be installed between the drawers, and how the drawer will be supported. If an old free-standing cabinet is to be converted to drawers, you can turn the entire unit over to the cabinet shop and have the drawers installed on the job.

Size: The minimum width of the cabinet opening should be 5 inches, if the drawer is to be used for general storage. Even with this width, the actual open drawer space will be only 3 3/4 inches wide, which is too narrow for many items. Drawers can be fitted into less width, but are usable only for storing specialty items, such as those found in a sewing center, bathroom vanity, or workshop. There are no minimum heights and depths for drawers; the only consideration should be weight of items stored in relation to size of the drawer bottom and method of supporting the units.

Materials: Though the drawer bottom is the only piece that will support a load, all parts of the drawer must be necessarily strong to keep the unit rigid and movable, even when loaded unevenly. Drawer bottoms can be 1/4-inch plywood if set in rabbets on the drawer front and sides and the drawer is not heavily loaded.

Drawer fronts are generally 3/4-inch stock, for appearance and to allow for 3/8-inch rabbets for lip fronts and some types of flush fronts. Sides and backs can

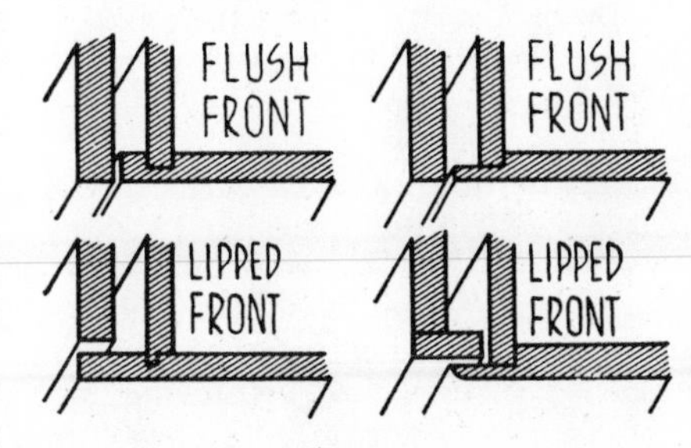

be 1/2-inch material, strong enough to hold the drawer rigid and not too thick to cut down on the actual usable drawer space; also, if the bottom is rabbeted into the sides, or you are using side guides, 1/2-inch material will take 1/4-inch rabbets and still be structually adequate.

Clearances: For a snug fit, allow 1/16-inch clearance between each drawer side and cabinet wall; this allows the drawer to slide smoothly into the opening, but keeps it secure on the glides and supports. A similar clearance between the drawer top and cabinet cross-rail will both ease operation and allow for any minor construction errors or sagging of the cabinet frame.

Slides and Runners: The usefulness of drawers depends a great deal on the workability of the slides and runners on which the drawer operates. The most efficient — and expensive — are metal guides. These are obtainable in regular or heavy-duty sizes, to hold all types of drawers.

There are two general types of wood guides that can be used with standard drawers. The first is a side guide, with a glide strip attached to the inside wall of the frame and slides in a rabbeted groove on the drawer side; this can be reversed,

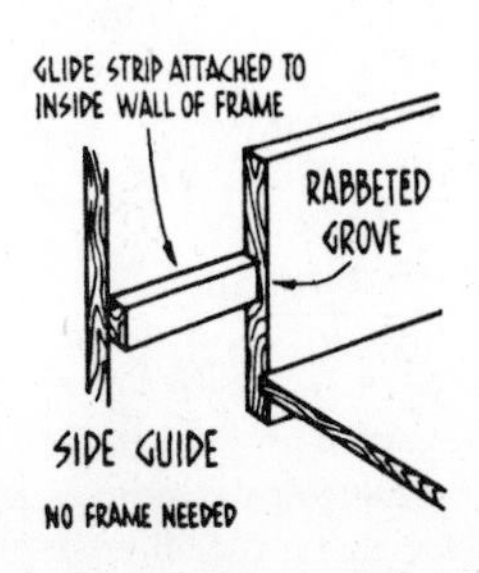

with the strip nailed to the drawer, and the groove dadoed into the cabinet frame.

Bottom guides are used where there is a front cross-rail to use as supporting frame. A channel 3/8-inch or 1/2-inch deep is set in the drawer bottom, and the glide strip is set between the front rail and the cabinet back, so it projects above the rail and fits in the drawer channel. For stability, mount the glide strip on a 3/4-inch by 3/4-inch piece of stock that will serve as a solid support and can be nailed firmly into the front cross-rail and cabinet back. This piece also will serve as a top support for the drawer immediately below. For the top drawer in a chest, install a similar piece of stock above the drawer opening to hold the drawer in place. The bottom drawer of a chest also needs special treatment if this type guide is used. Since the bottom unit will slide directly on the cabinet frame, it can be held in place simply by nailing 1/4-inch-square strips along the outside edges of the drawer sides.

Binding and Sticking: One of the most common complaints heard about wood drawers is that they will bind and stick. This is avoided with the use of metal guides; but wood moving on wood will bring a certain amount of binding that can be a nuisance and hamper the drawer's movement. To eliminate most of the binding, ease the edges of the wood guides and apply paraffin or wax; later, if the drawers begin to stick, a new application should eliminate the trouble.

Bins

Bins are handy storage units to have in the kitchen, utility room, bathroom, garage, or garden work center. They are ideal for bulk storage, as a laundry hamper, to store large quantities of dry foods, or to hold potting materials for garden work.

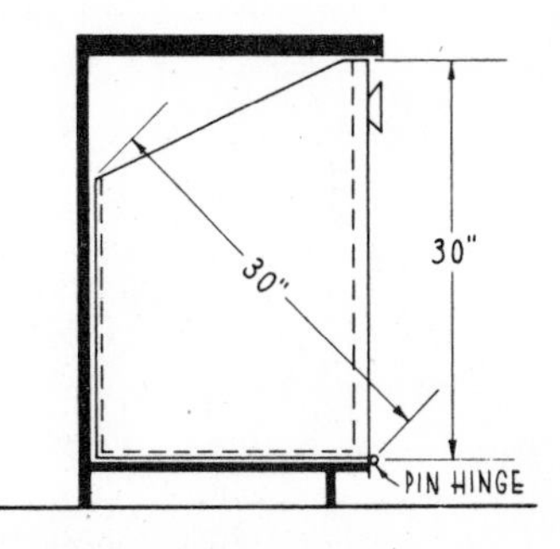

Main advantage of a bin is that it is easy to operate and exposes the full storage space when pulled open. You can reach the bottom of the bin easily and unload it with a minimum of effort. When closed, the bin keeps all items completely out of sight, yet easily accessible on a moment's notice.

Steel bins that fit under a kitchen sink are available, but only in limited styles and sizes. Since cabinet openings and depths vary, it is usually best to either have the bin made at a cabinet shop or make one yourself out of plywood. Half-inch material is satisfactory for the side and back pieces, and 3/4-inch will give the bin both a solid-looking and durable front. Build the bin sturdily to avoid having the front or back pull away when the bin is opened suddenly.

The principle of bin operation will work satisfactorily only when the height of the opening to be filled is greater than the depth. With equal dimensions or a greater depth than height, you will either have to insert a false back or design a special bin with slanted front; in either case, all of the cabinet space available will not be used, and drawers or slide-out shelves would probably be more valuable. With a cabinet opening of the proper dimensions, figuring the size of the bin is not difficult. Make a scale drawing of the cabinet opening; locate the hinge and measure the front height. With the hinge as a center point, use a compass to scribe an arc until it intersects with the back wall. The distance from this intersection to the cabinet bottom is the height of the back wall; also the compass arc determines the curvature of the sides so they will clear the opening when the bin is pulled out. If curved sides are not essential, cut the side pieces in a straight line from the top of the back to the top of the front.

The only other problem to be solved is how to keep the bin from falling out of the cabinet when it is opened. If the cabinet opening has a face frame projecting 3/4 or 1 inch into the opening, you have a built-in stop; make the back bin wall 1/2 or 3/4-inch higher than the clearance measurement, and it will hit the face frame and hold when the bin is opened. If this is done, be sure the side pieces are no higher than the previously determined intersection; if they are extended to the new back wall height, the sides will not clear the front opening and the bin will not open completely.

Without a projecting face frame, you can insert a 1/2 or 3/4-inch stop under the top rail. Nail it securely into the cabinet frame, as it will take repeated beatings as the bin is pulled open. Make the stop 1 1/2 inches shorter than the full opening width, to allow clearance for the sides. This way, the bin can be pulled open freely, but the back piece will hit the stop. When closed, the cabinet front will hide the stop.

Corners

Where two rows of wall or base cabinets meet in a corner of the kitchen, family room, or utility room, you are faced with the problem of how to use the corner space created. The convergence of two straight series of cabinets leaves a square opening, with little or no access into the room because of the projecting ends of cabinets adjacent to the corner.

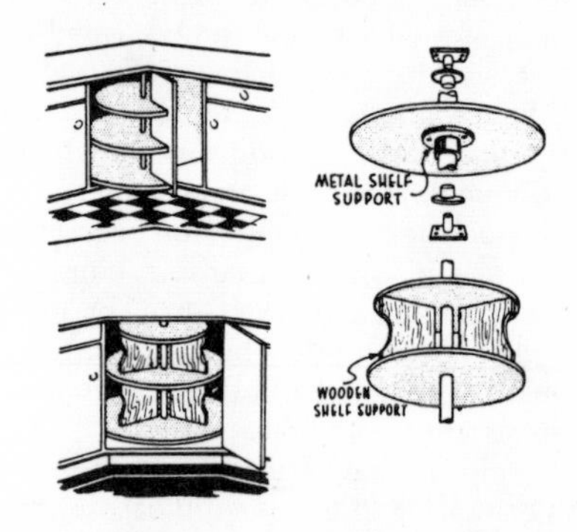

The most popular type of corner unit is the lazy susan, with revolving shelves that enable you to reach everything stored through a small door. The hardware is not expensive and installation in new cabinets is not difficult. You can inspect the larder at a glance and reach all items stored by revolving the unit. For shelves 24 inches in diameter, 33 inches along each wall is needed for clearance; 30-inch shelves require 36 inches along each wall.

Building between the studs

By utilizing the space between wall studs, you can often gain an extra storage cupboard without sacrificing any floor area.

Since the shelves in a between-the-studs cabinet are necessarily shallow, all storage is only one-deep, easy to see and easy to reach.

In choosing a spot for a between-the-studs cupboard, be sure it is far enough away from wall outlets or switches so you won't open up an area that contains electrical wiring.

Since the wall studs are usually built on 16-inch centers, you can often find them by measuring out from a corner of the room. However, some walls have extra studs near the corners, so it's also a good idea to look the wall over carefully for nailheads that tell you where the wall material is fastened to the studs.

If you are cutting into a plaster wall, cut an outline of the cupboard opening with a sharp knife. Cut as deeply into the plaster as you can, then chip off the plaster just inside the cut until you uncover the lath underneath. To cut into a wood or composition wall, first drill a hole large enough to insert a keyhole saw.

If you're planning to install a wide cupboard that calls for the removal of sections of more than 2 studs, it's a good idea to put props under the ceiling while you're cutting to take the load off the studs. Place a length of 2 by 4 against the ceiling several feet out from the wall, and prop it up with more 2 by 4's while you trim the studs and put in a header at the top of the cupboard to transfer the load to adjacent studs (see the sketch).

Many building codes require a 4 by 4-inch header for any wall span between 16 inches and 4 feet. In cutting away the studs, allow room for the header above the cupboard area and for a 2 by 4-inch foot at the bottom. Fasten "cripples" to the studs to support the header.

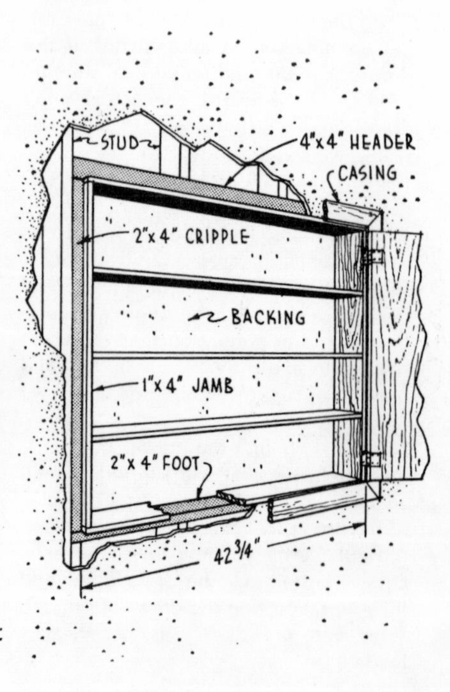